ADHD ORGANIZING MADE EASY

CONTROL THE CHAOS, ALLEVIATE STRESS, BOOST PRODUCTIVITY, AND ACHIEVE A LASTING CLUTTER-FREE LIFE

AMY MILLER

© **Copyright Amy Miller 2024 - All rights reserved.**

The content within this book may not be reproduced, duplicated or transmitted without direct written permission from the author or the publisher.

Under no circumstances will any blame or legal responsibility be held against the publisher, or author, for any damages, reparation, or monetary loss due to the information contained within this book. Either directly or indirectly. You are responsible for your own choices, actions, and results.

Legal Notice:

This book is copyright protected. This book is only for personal use. You cannot amend, distribute, sell, use, quote or paraphrase any part, of the content within this book, without the consent of the author or publisher.

Disclaimer Notice:

Please note the information contained within this document is for educational and entertainment purposes only. All effort has been expended to present accurate, up-to-date, and reliable, complete information. No warranties of any kind are declared or implied. Readers acknowledge that the author is not engaging in the rendering of legal, financial, medical or professional advice. The content within this book has been derived from various sources. Please consult a licensed professional before attempting any techniques outlined in this book.

By reading this document, the reader agrees that under no circumstances is the author responsible for any losses, direct or indirect, which are incurred as a result of the use of the information contained within this document, including, but not limited to, — errors, omissions, or inaccuracies.

First Printing 2024

Today I choose calm over chaos,
serenity over stress,
peace over perfection,
grace over grit,
faith over fear.

Mary Davis

CONTENTS

Introduction   7

1. Understand Your ADHD and Organization   11
2. What Is Your Clutter Personality?   25
3. Create a Personalized Plan   35
4. Master Time Management and Prioritization   45
5. Conquer Clutter: Physical and Digital   57
6. Enhance Productivity and Reduce Stress   79
7. Build Long-Lasting Habits   91

Conclusion   113
References   117

INTRODUCTION

Your day begins with a rush. You glance around and see the chaos: dishes in the sink, papers piled, clothes in heaps, and digital notifications piling up. You start to feel overwhelmed. For many adults and young adults with ADHD(Attention-deficit/hyperactivity disorder), this scene is all too common. Organizing feels like a never-ending battle, one that leaves you exhausted and defeated before you even start.

This book is here to offer you a different path. Its purpose is to provide practical, actionable strategies tailored for adults and young adults with ADHD. You will find ways to organize your life, reduce stress, and boost your productivity. The goal is not just to tidy up, but to transform your daily experience from clutter to calm.

The journey we are about to take together is a transformative one. By adopting simple, effective habits, you can shift from feeling overwhelmed to feeling in control. This book envisions a life where organization is not a burden, but instead, a tool for creating peace and efficiency.

You are the target audience for this book. You, who want easy steps to reduce clutter and improve time management. You, who seek lasting success in organizing your life. Whether you struggle with physical mess or digital overload, this book speaks to your needs.

What sets this book apart is identifying your Clutter Personality and then focusing on both physical and digital decluttering. The strategies are designed with ADHD-friendly formats, making them easy to implement.

The challenges you face are real. Clutter can feel overwhelming, time management seems elusive, and motivation often fluctuates. These pain points are not just acknowledged here; they are addressed with practical solutions.

Let me share a bit about myself. I am a business woman, wife, mother, quilter, athlete, and I am creative to the core. I used to believe that all creative people with ADHD were messy like me and that there was no hope. Through years of struggling with organizing my life in all of my roles, I have developed a deep passion for helping myself and others find peace through organization. I am committed to providing guidance that is not only practical but also easy to follow. My experience has shown me the profound impact that organization can have on reducing stress and improving quality of life.

The structure of this book is carefully crafted to guide you through this journey. It begins with understanding ADHD and its impact on organization. From there, it moves into finding what kind of Clutter Personality applies to you. Then we move into actionable strategies for integrating organization into your daily life. Each chapter builds upon the last, creating a cohesive and empowering experience. At the end of the book you will find a

Bonus QR code that takes you to printables that you can use on your organization journey.

As you read, expect a hands-on approach. The book offers simple, effective habits that can lead to significant improvements in your life. You will find tips that are easy to apply and adaptable to your unique situation.

I want to inspire and motivate you as we conclude this introduction. Embrace the journey of transformation that lies ahead. Believe in your ability to create a clutter-free, productive life. Change is possible, and it starts with small, manageable steps. Together, we will move from chaos to calm, and you will find the peace and productivity you deserve.

1

UNDERSTAND YOUR ADHD AND ORGANIZATION

One of my core memories as a child of the tender age of 8 or 9 was my mom standing at the door to my bedroom calling for me. "AMY! Are you in there?" As I awoke with a start, I popped my head up and slammed it into a metal bar…underneath my bed. She had told me to clean my room and my usual cleaning method consisted of shoving everything under the bed so that the mess could not be seen. This time my mom got a little wiser and demanded that I clean under the bed as well. As you can imagine, I became overwhelmed pretty quickly once I crawled under the bed surrounded by clutter and I laid my head down for just a minute. A minute turned into hours and that's how I found myself with a sore head and a still messy, unorganized bedroom. Have you ever found yourself staring at a messy room, feeling frozen, unsure where to start? The clutter around you feels like the chaos inside your mind. This is a common scene for those with ADHD. Often, the clutter is more than just physical; it's a reflection of the internal challenges that make organizing seem daunting. Understanding these challenges is the first step toward effective organization.

ADHD affects various brain functions that are crucial for organization. The prefrontal cortex, the brain's command center, plays an essential role in planning, decision-making, and impulse control. For someone with ADHD, this area can function differently, leading to executive function challenges (Executive function is a set of higher-level cognitive skills that help people manage their thoughts, emotions, and actions to achieve goals). These challenges affect your ability to prioritize tasks, manage time, and initiate actions. Imagine trying to start an engine that sputters and stalls. That's what task initiation can feel like. You know what needs to be done, but getting started is another matter entirely.

1.1 THE ADHD BRAIN: HOW IT INFLUENCES YOUR ORGANIZATIONAL SKILLS

The executive function challenges of the ADHD brain often show up as difficulties in organizing and planning. The prefrontal cortex, a critical region responsible for these skills, might not work as well in those with ADHD. This inefficiency can lead to problems with impulse control. You might find yourself acting on a whim, grabbing items you don't need, or starting tasks without a plan. This impulsivity can clutter both your physical spaces and your schedule. Task initiation is another hurdle. Knowing what to do and actually doing it are worlds apart. It's like being stuck at the starting line, unable to take the first step.

Hyperfocus, a term you might be familiar with, is both a blessing and a curse. When channeled correctly, it can be a powerful tool for organizing. You may lose yourself in a task, ignoring everything else, which can be incredibly productive. However, hyperfocus can often attach itself to non-prioritized tasks, like deep-cleaning a closet when you should be preparing for a meeting. The key is to learn how to direct this intense focus toward organizing sessions. Imagine tackling a cluttered desk with laser-like precision, turning chaos into order in record time. The challenge lies in harnessing hyperfocus deliberately, not letting it choose your tasks for you.

Time blindness is another aspect that complicates organization for those with ADHD. It's the tendency to struggle with perceiving time accurately. You may underestimate how long a task will take or forget deadlines altogether. This misjudgment leads to overcommitment, as you believe you have more time than you actually do. Consequently, tasks pile up, and stress levels rise. Understanding and addressing time blindness can improve your task management. Tools like timers, alarms, and visual schedules can help anchor your perception of time, providing structure in what often feels like a timeless void.

Despite these challenges, ADHD also brings unique strengths to organizing. The creative and out-of-the-box thinking often associated with ADHD can lead to innovative storage solutions. You might find yourself devising clever ways to maximize space, seeing possibilities that others overlook. This creativity allows for non-linear task engagement, meaning that you can tackle tasks in unconventional, yet effective ways. Embracing these strengths can transform the organizing process from a rigid set of rules to a dynamic and personalized system. You have the ability to view organization through a different lens, one that allows flexibility and creativity to thrive. Consider it a superpower that, when understood and applied, can turn the organizing process into an art form that reflects your unique perspective.

1.2 COMMON MISCONCEPTIONS ABOUT ADHD AND CLUTTER

It's a myth that ADHD always means disorganization. This stereotype has been pushed by media portrayals and misunderstandings, painting all individuals with ADHD with the same broad brush. The truth is, organizational capabilities among those with ADHD are as diverse as the individuals themselves. Just because you have ADHD doesn't mean that you CAN'T be organized. In fact, many people with ADHD develop unique strategies that work exceptionally well for them. These strategies often involve adapting traditional methods to fit your own needs, illustrating that organization is indeed possible and personal.

Clutter is not synonymous with chaos, nor is it a definitive trait of ADHD. Instead, it can be a symptom of the underlying issues related to this condition. For many, clutter serves as a coping mechanism for anxiety, providing a distraction from internal turmoil. Conversely, the physical act of organizing can serve as a coping mechanism for needing structure to feel calm. Emotional attachment to items is another factor, where objects hold sentimental value that makes them hard to part with. This attachment can create clutter, but it doesn't mean disorganization by default. Recognizing this distinction is crucial. Clutter is something that can be managed, not a permanent state of being. Understanding why clutter accumulates can be the first step in addressing it, allowing you to create spaces that truly reflect your needs and preferences.

The misconception that organizing is impossible for those with ADHD is simply not true. Numerous success stories demonstrate that organization is achievable. For example, statistics show that with the right strategies, individuals with ADHD can match or even surpass the organizational skills of their peers. The key lies in finding methods that complement your unique way of thinking and working.

1.3 IDENTIFY YOUR PERSONAL ORGANIZING STRENGTHS

Reflecting on your natural abilities can be a powerful exercise, especially when it feels like everything is working against you. With ADHD, you might often focus on what's challenging, rather than recognizing where you naturally excel. It's time to shift that perspective. Begin by considering your strengths. Think about times when organizing came a bit easier to you, or even felt enjoyable. Journaling can be an effective tool for this self-assessment. Spend a few minutes each day writing about what organizational tasks felt manageable and why. Perhaps you found success using a particular method or tool. By documenting these moments, you start to see patterns in your abilities. Another source of valuable insight is feedback from friends and family. They might notice strengths that you might overlook. Listen closely to their observations. They can offer a fresh perspective on your organizing capabilities, highlighting skills you may have taken for granted.

Your interests and passions hold significant potential in driving organizational success. They can transform seemingly boring tasks into fun activities. If you're passionate about art, for example, organizing your supplies can become an enjoyable project rather than a chore. Hobbies can be seamlessly integrated into your organizational tasks, turning them into opportunities for creativity and expression. Passion projects provide motivation, making it easier to stay committed to your goals. When you align organizational tasks with your interests, you create a sense of purpose that fuels your efforts. This approach also allows you to tailor organizing methods to fit your unique needs, resulting in systems that are both effective and enjoyable to maintain.

ADHD traits, often viewed negatively, can actually be leveraged to your advantage in organizing. Rapid adaptability, for instance, allows you to pivot and adjust your methods quickly if something isn't working. This flexibility can lead to innovative solutions that others might not consider. High energy bursts, common in those with ADHD, can be harnessed for intense, focused organizing sessions. These bursts of energy can help you tackle tasks that require significant effort in short, manageable periods. By recognizing and embracing these traits, you can develop organizational strategies that align with your natural tendencies, making the process more intuitive and less overwhelming.

Developing a personalized organizing style is key to creating systems that work for you. One-size-fits-all solutions rarely meet the needs of individuals with ADHD. Instead, focus on tailoring methodologies that suit your strengths and preferences. This might involve experimenting with different approaches, such as visual organization, or digital tools, to find what resonates best. Custom storage solutions can also play a crucial role in your strategy. Consider your daily routines and how your spaces function. Design storage options that align with these routines, ensuring that everything has a designated place. By creating systems that reflect your personal style, you increase the likelihood of maintaining them over time, building a foundation for lasting organizational success.

1.4 EMBRACE THE CHAOS: WHY DISORDER ISN'T ALWAYS BAD

The notion of chaos often conjures images of disarray and confusion, yet within this apparent disorder lies a wealth of creativity and innovation. For many adults with ADHD, what appears as chaos is fertile ground for spontaneous ideas. Consider your workspace: a jumble of notes, pens, and gadgets may seem overwhelming to some, but to others, it's an environment ripe for potential. Creative workspace environments allow for the free flow of your ideas without the constraints of rigid order. This is where innovation thrives, as your mind, unencumbered by strict organization, explores possibilities and connections that might otherwise remain hidden. The spontaneity that comes with a bit of disorder can lead to those eureka moments, where your solutions or insights emerge seemingly out of nowhere.

Finding the balance between chaos and organization is crucial. Controlled chaos, if you will, can coexist with effective organization, creating a dynamic system that is both adaptable and efficient. Flexible organizing systems accommodate the ebb and flow of creative energy, allowing for periods of disorder where necessary, but also providing structure when the time comes to focus and execute tasks. Adaptive task management is the key here, where priorities shift as needed, and tasks are organized in a way that aligns with your current state of mind. This flexibility means that while your environment may not always appear neat, it functions optimally for your specific needs and processes, supporting both productivity and creativity.

Throughout history, numerous individuals have thrived in what others might deem chaotic conditions. Albert Einstein, known for his unparalleled contributions to science, was famously indifferent to the clutter on his desk. He once remarked, "If a cluttered desk is a sign of a cluttered mind, of what, then, is an empty desk a sign?" Einstein's workspace, filled with papers and books, was a testament to the idea that creativity often requires a departure from strict order. The clutter was not indicative of a lack of organization, but rather, a reflection of a mind engaged in complex thought. His example suggests that a certain level of disorder can facilitate a depth of thinking and creativity that rigid organization may stifle.

Accepting a degree of disorder is not about resigning yourself to chaos, but about acknowledging that perfection is neither necessary nor always desirable. Emphasizing functionality over aesthetics can lead to more practical and sustainable organizing practices. A space that functions well for its intended purpose, even if it lacks visual perfection, can serve you far better than one that prioritizes appearance over utility. This sensible approach allows you a more realistic and compassionate view of your environment, reducing the pressure to conform to unrealistic standards of tidiness. It fosters an atmosphere where your creativity can flourish, free from the constraints of maintaining an immaculate facade.

Creative Workspace Exercise

Take a moment to observe your workspace. What items inspire creativity or prompt new ideas? Consider rearranging your space to highlight these elements, allowing them to play a central role in your environment. Reflect on how your current setup supports or hinders your creative processes. Adjust as needed to find a balance that sparks innovation while providing the structure necessary for productivity. Embrace the chaos, but guide it with intention.

1.5 THE EMOTIONAL TOLL OF CLUTTER AND HOW TO ADDRESS IT

Clutter doesn't just occupy physical space; it occupies mental and emotional space too. For those with ADHD, the sight of piles and disorder can trigger a cascade of stress responses, escalating into anxiety or depression. The clutter becomes a constant reminder of tasks left undone, of goals unmet, amplifying feelings of inadequacy. Every item out of place can symbolize a task waiting to be tackled, and this perpetual to-do list can wear down your mental health. Anxiety often arises from this chaos, creating a cycle where clutter leads to stress, and stress leads to more clutter. Your mind craves order, yet finds itself trapped in a disorganized reality.

To break free from this cycle, practical strategies are essential. Mindfulness exercises can help mitigate the emotional effects of clutter. When anxiety mounts, pause and take a few deep breaths, grounding yourself in the present moment. This simple act can reduce stress and clear your mind, allowing you to approach your space with a fresh perspective. Engaging in stress-reduction techniques, like progressive muscle relaxation or guided imagery, can also provide relief. These practices help calm the nervous system, reducing the emotional burden clutter imposes. By managing stress, you are setting the stage for more effective organization.

Your emotional attachment to objects often complicates decluttering efforts. Items accumulate sentimental value, representing memories, relationships, or aspirations. Letting go becomes a daunting task, not merely a physical act but an emotional release. Assess the sentimental value of items and weigh it against the space they occupy. Consider the joy or utility they bring to your life now. Emotional decluttering exercises, such as writing about an item's significance, can aid in this process. This reflection helps detach emotions from objects, making it easier for you to part with them. It's not about discarding your memories; it's about preserving them in a way that doesn't overwhelm your space.

Clutter, in many ways, tells a story. It reflects your personality, your habits, and even your state of mind. Consider viewing clutter as a form of self-expression. Each pile, each misplaced item, holds a narrative. Clutter journaling can be an insightful exercise. Document what your clutter says about you. Is it a collection of unfinished projects indicating your creative pursuits? Or perhaps it's a testament to your readiness for the next adventure, with bags half-packed and ready to go. Through this lens, your clutter becomes more than a mess; it becomes a window into your world. Understanding this story can offer you surprising clarity.

Emotional Decluttering Exercise

Take a moment to identify an item that you are emotionally attached to. Write down its story. Reflect on why it's significant and how it fits into your life now. Consider whether keeping it supports your current goals or if letting it go could pave the way for new experiences. Use this exercise to guide your decisions, balancing sentiment with practicality.

1.6 ADHD-FRIENDLY ORGANIZING FORMATS: MAKE INFORMATION WORK FOR YOU

When you live with ADHD, traditional organizing methods may feel like trying to fit a square peg into a round hole. Your brain craves systems that are intuitive, engaging, and adaptable to the way it processes information. Bullet-point checklists are a powerful tool in this regard. They break down tasks into bite-sized pieces, making them easier to tackle and less overwhelming. By visually separating tasks, checklists provide clarity and a sense of accomplishment with each box checked. Checklists serve as a roadmap, guiding you through daily responsibilities. In a similar way, color-coded systems can transform chaos into a visually appealing space. Assigning specific colors to categories or priorities can help your brain to instantly recognize and differentiate between tasks, reducing the cognitive load of sorting through information. This simple yet effective strategy can be applied to everything from filing systems to digital calendars, creating an organized rainbow that is pleasing to the eye and easy for you to navigate.

Visual aids and cues are indispensable allies in your quest for organization. Imagine walking into a room and immediately seeing a visual task board that outlines your priorities for the day. This board serves as a constant, gentle reminder of what needs your attention, reducing the reliance on your memory alone. It acts as both a motivator and an accountability partner, holding you to your commitments in a tangible way. Labeling systems further enhance this visual strategy. By clearly marking where items belong, labels eliminate the guesswork and ensure that everything has a home. This not only streamlines the process of finding and storing items, but also reinforces habits of returning things to their designated spots. The simplicity of labels belies their effectiveness, providing a straightforward solution to your maintaining order.

Simplicity is the cornerstone of any successful organizing system, especially for those with ADHD. Simplified filing systems cut through the clutter of complexity, offering you a direct path to information retrieval. By reducing the number of categories and subcategories, you free yourself from the mental gymnastics of trying to remember where something might be filed. This reductionist approach can also be applied to your task lists. Streamlined lists prioritize what's critical, presenting a manageable number of tasks for you to focus on at a time. This ensures that your attention is directed toward meaningful activities, minimizing distractions and enhancing your productivity.

In today's digital age, technology offers a treasure trove of tools tailored to the ADHD mind. Apps like Trello and Todoist stand out as versatile platforms for task management. They allow you to organize tasks visually, using boards, lists, and cards to represent projects and responsibilities. These digital tools offer flexibility in how information is structured and accessed, accommodating the ebb and flow of your productivity. Digital calendars with reminders are another essential component of an ADHD-friendly toolkit. They act as an external memory bank, prompting you about upcoming deadlines, appointments, and tasks. By offloading the responsibility of remembering to technology, you create mental space for creativity and focus.

These ADHD-friendly organizing formats are not just about tidying up your physical or digital surroundings. They are about creating systems that resonate with the way your brain works, enhancing comprehension and retention. By integrating these strategies into daily life, you can build a framework that supports your unique needs and promotes a sense of order and control.

1.7 BUILD THE RIGHT MINDSET: FROM OVERWHELMED TO EMPOWERED

Imagine waking up each day with a sense of purpose, rather than dread. The key to overcoming organizational hurdles lies in cultivating a growth mindset. This mindset embraces challenges and sees them as opportunities to learn and improve. When you shift your perspective from "I can't" to "I can learn," you open the door to progress. The journey to organization is full of small victories that deserve celebration. Each drawer you tidy, and each file you sort, becomes a triumph. Recognizing these achievements, no matter how minor they seem, builds momentum and confidence. Mistakes, too, are part of this process. Instead of viewing them as failures, see them as stepping stones to your success. Each misstep teaches you something valuable, shaping a path forward that's more informed and resilient.

Keeping motivation alive can sometimes feel like a full-time job, and yet, with the right techniques and strategies, it becomes manageable. Setting clear, attainable goals provides direction and focus. Break down your larger aspirations into smaller, actionable steps. This creates a roadmap to guide you through the chaos, one task at a time. Reward systems can further enhance your motivation. Reward yourself when you complete a task, whether it's a small treat or a moment of relaxation. These incentives encourage continued effort and reinforce positive behaviors, making organization an enjoyable endeavor rather than a chore.

Self-compassion is crucial throughout this journey. It's easy to fall into the trap of self-criticism when things don't go as planned. Instead, practice positive self-talk. Remind yourself of your strengths and the progress that you have already made. This kindness toward yourself can foster a supportive inner environment where your growth can flourish. Self-reflection practices, such as journaling or quiet contemplation, can help you understand your experiences and emotions better. By nurturing a deep sense of self-awareness, you empower yourself to make informed decisions that align with your values and goals.

Empowerment comes from taking control of your organizational efforts. Personal accountability tools, like daily planners or accountability partners, keep you on track. They serve as gentle reminders of your commitments, helping you to stay focused and diligent. Success tracking methods, such as progress charts or visual boards, allow you to see how far you've come. These tools not only provide motivation, but also offer a clear view of your achievements, building confidence in your ability to manage your space effectively. With each step you take, you reclaim your environment, turning it into a place of calm and order.

This mindset transformation is not just about organizing your physical space, but also about organizing your thoughts and emotions. It's about creating harmony between your inner and outer worlds. As you continue this process, remember that empowerment is not a destination, but a state of being. By embracing a growth mindset, you cultivate resiliency and adaptability. You learn to navigate challenges with grace and confidence. This mindset becomes a powerful ally, guiding you toward a life that is not just organized, but also fulfilling. You hold the power to shape your surroundings and, in doing so, to shape your life.

2

WHAT IS YOUR CLUTTER PERSONALITY?

This entire chapter is devoted to figuring out what type of Clutter Personality best matches the way you naturally operate. By identifying the natural way that you behave, you can find solutions that work specifically for you. This is a general guide. You may identify with more than one type of Clutter Personality, and that's completely normal. Just try to think about how the solutions presented can create the most solutions for your life.

2.1 THE VISUAL

This type of person likes to see all of their belongings and worries. If these belongings are put away, they might not remember to use them. These individuals like to have visual reminders and struggle to put things away. You are probably a Visual clutterer if you have piles of clothes on the floor and papers on the desk, but only a few clothes in the closet, and only a few papers filed.

Visual clutterers get overwhelmed with the idea of organizing and don't know where to begin, so they put off the task entirely. They can also become easily distracted and move from one project to the next, rarely finishing any of them. These individuals need to be careful that the things they leave out don't overrun their homes, stealing precious time and energy from the ones they love.

Visual clutterers are usually fun, energetic, and highly creative people. Once their space is organized in a way that works for them, they take pride in keeping it beautiful for themselves and their families.

Here are some quick tips on organizing for Visuals:

- CLEAR BINS are perfect for putting things away while still being able to see the contents. Since the contents are still visible, you are more likely to keep using them.
- LABEL EVERYTHING! You can use words or pictures to always have a visual reminder of the contents. If in doubt, label it. You can find inexpensive label makers online. My favorite label maker is the Dymo Letratag 200B, because it's wireless, compact, and it can be used through a phone app. Use clearly labeled baskets and bins for your office, pantry, closet, or just about everywhere. Studies show that you are three times more likely to put something away if it has a labeled bin where it belongs.
- DRY ERASE BOARDS are perfect for organizing your schedule. This is a great way to organize in a visible way. You can make to-do lists, schedule family events, work events, workouts, etc. Other similar ideas are blackboards, corkboards, or even digital organizers, as long as they are put in a prominent place where you will see them.
- ASK FOR HELP. For bigger organization projects, consider having a friend or family member help, since it is hard for

you to recognize your own clutter. Have friends help you sort what needs to be donated or tossed. Once things are in organized bins, you and your helper can put them away.
- SORTING METHOD to organize your spaces. Take four labeled and colored baskets: TRASH, DONATE, MOVE TO ANOTHER ROOM, and KEEP. Continue to sort one room until the space is done. Visuals can tend to become distracted so try to stay on task until the space is sorted completely or set a timer and sort until the timer goes off. If the task is not done, schedule to move the task to the next available day in your schedule. Continue to do this until the task is completed.
- CREATE A VISION PICTURE. Visuals are motivated by beauty. Take a picture of the current room. Then try to find a picture of what you want your space to look like when the job is done, placing it in a prominent area of the room. This should help you stay on track.
- 30 MINUTES OF ORGANIZATION: Schedule organizing time each and every day. 15 Minutes of organization in the morning and 15 minutes at night is best. Try to organize the same time every day so you create a habit. Don't forget to set a timer. Once you are done, move on to the rest of your life.
- PURGE: Every month set aside a time to purge. Consider what you have purchased in the month and decide if you can get rid of a similar item that you already own that needs repair, doesn't fit, or can be donated. I call this the "One-for-One Method". If you bought one, give or throw one away that is no longer needed, you don't love it or find it to be beautiful. This will make the space to see all the things you truly love and cherish.
- OPEN SHELVING is your friend. Not only can you see everything you have, but it forces you to organize the

things you have to make it more aesthetically pleasing. If you are going to spend money on organizing, let it be shelving, bins, and labeling.
- PEOPLE ARE MOST IMPORTANT. People are more important than things. Don't let stuff overwhelm you to the point that you can't enjoy your family and friends. By getting rid of clutter you can create better experiences for your family and loved ones while improving your quality of life.
- REWARD YOURSELF with something that fills your bucket. Invite the friend who helped you sort over for lunch or coffee to show off your newly calmed and organized space.

2.2 THE PERFECTIONIST

The perfectionist is a classic piler. The piles are probably neat and tidy but still piles. You may think that perfectionists would not have trouble with organization, but this is not always the case. Perfectionists feel that if they can't do something perfectly, why bother doing it at all. This personality type can take too much time setting up the method, or they can create a system that is too complex to easily use, which can lead to a lot of incomplete to-do piles that can easily get out of control.

The best solution for this type of personality is to let go of perfection while learning to be OK with functional and good enough. Creating a system that works to minimize clutter today is better than a perfect system tomorrow (which never comes because there is no time to create the perfect system).

- SORT PAPERS. Vertical files are easily visible. Take all of your piles of papers and sort them by groups: Urgent,

Important, and Not Important etc., **but file** (this could be manuals,etc). These are the only files you keep vertically. Once a week, minimum, deal with the papers in these files (pay the bills, get questions answered, schedule appointments related to the paperwork), and then move them to the scan and shred category. Don't let these sit for more than a week.

- SCAN and SHRED. When clearing out the vertical files, you can sort further by groups: Medical, Mortgage, Insurance, etc. After you've sorted your papers, scan and then shred them. Just make sure that when you scan them, you save them to the appropriate file or you will be making digital clutter, which is not the goal here.
- LABEL EVERYTHING. If in doubt, label it. Make sure the labels are clear and easy to read, and stick with one type of font. As noted earlier, my favorite label maker is the Dymo Letratag 200B, because it's wireless, compact, and it can be used through a phone app.
- MAKE LISTS and Check them off. Any kind of list you use is fine. Your list can be paper, digital, white board, etc. The key is that you **use it**.
- REMOVE DISTRACTIONS. Before you set your timer to start your task, remove distractions. You may need to silence your phone, remove your smart watch, turn off social media, put on classical music, or put on noise cancelling headphones. Do whatever it takes to create the traction it takes to get the job done.
- TIMERS are your friend. Make sure that you pick a realistic time goal - 15 to 30 minutes to get the job done and feel the accomplishment.
- BASKETS are a good choice as long as they have open tops so you can see when they become full. If the basket is full, empty it. Tie this to any other habit that you have.

- GOOD ENOUGH is GREAT! Perfection leads to jobs left undone.

2.3 THE HIDERS

Hiders really benefit from short bursts of timed cleaning and organizing. You can pick one area that you know is a hidden clutter zone, and get to sorting. We will discuss this method in depth later. I can really relate with this section as I am a classic Hider. When we were newly married, my husband used to say he loved it when we invited people over because the whole house got cleaned. It would take us forever to find the things I "cleaned" because all the mess was hidden somewhere, but the common areas were spotless.

Here are some quick tips on organizing for Hiders.

- EASY IS KEY: Make it easy to put things away. Designate a "place" for every item. If you get a new item, consider giving the old one away. Make sure that the new item has a home, and that it is labeled or designated as such.
- DRAWER ORGANIZATION is mandatory. Deep drawers need taller organization or they will just become a jumbled mess. You will find this especially true in bathrooms where products are different sizes and shapes. If you are finding it hard to organize these drawers, try bins. Your items should fit standing up in bins, If not, use multiple layers of trays and lay them down. For shallow drawers, especially in kitchens, use dividers and trays to keep everything sorted and in its place.
- CLEAR BINS that are open on top make it easy to place an item, but it will still feel like it's hidden and contained.

- BINDERS can be great for you. Put the contents in clear plastic sleeves where they are easily accessible and organized. Be sure to label the outside of the binder, or color code it, so that the contents are easy to find.
- BEAUTIFUL CONTAINERS are perfect for storing something in an area that must be seen. If you love beautiful, tidy spaces, it's easier to put things away in a container that is beautiful. Consider different shapes or colors to designate what's inside, or just put a pretty label on it. You are more likely to use it if it's obvious to everyone as to what's Inside.
- 30 MINUTES OF ORGANIZATION: Schedule organizing time each and every day. 15 Minutes of organization in the morning and 15 minutes at night is best. Try to organize the same time every day so you create a habit. Don't forget to set a timer! Once you are done, you can move on to the rest of your life.
- INTUITIVE ORGANIZING: Make sure that you have a place for the items that you use, where you actually use them. Let's say you have a craft room, but your kids use markers, scissors, glue sticks, and colored pencils at the kitchen table, where they do their homework. It makes sense to have a storage bin in the kitchen area to contain the items since they will be used in more than one location. Likewise, if you stretch your back in your living room with a foam roller, make sure that there's a bin in your living room for your bodywork tools.

2.4 THE ACCUMULATOR

This personality type enjoys experiencing it all. They have many projects and hobbies at the same time, and like to keep things out until they finish. You know you are an Accumulator if you have lots of everything. Whatever job, hobby, or passion you have at the time, becomes mounds of stuff that need to go with it. This stuff gets difficult to contain with the sheer volume of interests creating clutter, which can zap the peace and calm from your home.

Here are some quick tips on organization for Accumulators:

- MINIMIZE THE VOLUME OF PROJECTS: Try to have no more than a few projects going at any time. Three is a good number.
- PURGE: Accumulators tend to get super excited about a project, then move on to the next "super fun" project while the original one goes unfinished, taking up space, and creating clutter. Consider giving the unfinished project to someone who will finish it and appreciate the challenge. By giving a project away, you can feel good about decluttering while the person you are donating it to will appreciate the gift. Also, consider the sheer number of things you have. Do you need three vegetable peelers (even if they do function slightly differently than the others)? Space constraints will help you decide in many cases. If it doesn't have a permanent home, sort it into a donation or trash bin.
- THINK BEFORE YOU JUMP: Before you jump into a new project, consider how many projects you have ongoing, and remember your max of three projects at any one time. If you already have three projects going, finish one before you start a new one, or donate the old one to someone else before starting the new project.
- PRIORITIZE: Make a list of what is truly important to you. Complete that task before starting a new one.
- THE ONE YEAR RULE: Accumulators like to keep things, just in case they might need them some day. "Those jeans

might fit me if I ever lose 10 lbs," or "This piece for something I no longer use might fit something else someday". If you haven't used it in a year, sort it and remove it from your life. You don't need it! Make room for the things you love and actually use.
- USE A PLANNER: Accumulators want to get so much accomplished, but much of it will go undone without the use of a planner. There are various options: Daily, Weekly, Monthly, Yearly, Paper, Binder, or Digital. It really doesn't matter which option.

3

CREATE A PERSONALIZED PLAN

P icture yourself standing at the entrance of your home, taking a deep breath, ready to reclaim your space. The clutter has become a silent companion, whispering doubt and distraction. Yet, beneath the surface clutter lies the potential for a peaceful home organized to meet your unique aesthetic and needs. This chapter is about unlocking that potential and turning your living space into a reflection of your goals. By systematically assessing each room, you can transform even the most cluttered corners into areas of calm and functionality. It's time for you to move beyond the generic organizational tips that never quite fit, and create a plan that truly resonates with you.

3.1 ROOM BY ROOM INVENTORY: LOOK FOR HOT SPOTS

Begin by taking a comprehensive look at each room. This detailed inventory is your first step toward understanding where the clutter accumulates and why. Walk through your home with fresh eyes, pretending that you're seeing it for the first time. Identify

Hot Spots: those areas where items tend to pile up, like the kitchen counter, closets, drawers, or the entryway table. These zones often signal underlying issues in your organizing system. Is there enough storage? Are items easy to access? Note underutilized spaces too, like shelves, or corners, that could serve a better purpose. These observations will become the groundwork for your personalized plan.

Noting your findings is crucial. It helps track progress and can keep you accountable. Consider using the _**Room-By-Room Inventory Checklist**_ that I've created for you in the Bonus Chapter at the end of the book. List each room and jot down specific problem areas and ideas for improvement. Photography can be an invaluable tool here. Snap photos of each room and note your thoughts on improvements that could be made. This snapshot works as both a reminder of where you started, and a motivator, as you make changes. With each image, you can see, not only the clutter, but also the possibility of a better, clutter free organized life.

As you analyze your space, consider both challenges and opportunities. Every room has unique characteristics that can be leveraged to your advantage. Natural lighting, for example, can highlight certain areas, making them ideal for displaying items that you love. A well-lit corner might become the perfect reading nook, with just a comfy chair and a small bookshelf. Think about the layout and how it affects your traffic flow. Are there areas where you frequently trip or struggle to move around? These spots might benefit from a different arrangement, or the removal of unnecessary items. Each room has the potential to be both functional and inviting.

Understanding the functionality of each room is key. A room's setup should align with its intended purpose. Consider a multi-purpose room solution if space is limited. A guest room can double as a home office with the addition of a fold-away desk and a convertible sofa bed. This flexibility can ensure that every square inch of space is serving your needs, reducing clutter, and maximizing functionality. Think about how you use each room daily, and adjust the layout to support these activities. The more purposeful the space, the easier it will be to maintain order.

Below are some things to consider when doing your Room-by-Room Inventory:

1. **Purpose and Functionality**
   - Define the Purpose of the Space: Determine the primary activities for the area (e.g., working, relaxing, eating) to tailor its organization.
   - Ease of Access: Arrange items based on frequency of use. Frequently used items should be easily accessible, while less-used items can be stored away.
   - Zoning: Divide the space into functional zones (e.g., a reading nook, a workspace, or a play area).
2. **Decluttering**
   - Eliminate Excess: Remove items that no longer serve a purpose or bring joy, to reduce visual clutter.
   - Storage Solutions: Use bins, baskets, or cabinets to keep necessary items organized and out of sight.
3. **Storage and Organization**
   - Adequate Storage: Look for opportunities to add shelves, cabinets, or multi-purpose furniture with built-in storage.
   - Labeling: Use labels for containers or bins, to ensure that everything has a designated place.
   - Vertical Space: Maximize wall space with hooks, shelves, or pegboard.

4. **Flow and Layout**
   - **Clear Pathways:** Ensure that the layout promotes movement without obstacles.
   - **Furniture Placement:** Arrange furniture to enhance natural flow and encourage interaction, such as placing chairs to face one another.
5. **Lighting**
   - **Natural Light:** Optimize the use of natural light by keeping windows unobstructed.
   - **Layered Lighting:** Use a mix of overhead lighting, task lights, and ambient lighting to create a warm and functional atmosphere.
6. **Comfort and Aesthetics**
   - **Cozy Elements:** Add soft textures like rugs, cushions, or throws to make the space more inviting.
   - **Personal Touches:** Incorporate personal items like family photos, artwork, or decorative pieces that reflect your personality.
   - **Color Palette:** Choose colors that promote the mood you want to set, such as calming tones for bedrooms, and vibrant colors for play areas.
7. **Flexibility**
   - **Multi-Functional Spaces:** Use furniture or decor that can serve multiple purposes, such as a sofa bed, or a dining room table, that doubles as workspace.
   - **Adjustability:** Consider adjustable shelves, modular furniture, or movable storage for your changing needs.
8. **Sustainability**
   - **Eco-Friendly Choices:** Use sustainable materials and repurpose existing items.
   - **Low Maintenance:** Opt for finishes and materials that are easy to clean and maintain.

9. **Accessibility**
    - **Inclusive Design:** Ensure that the space is functional for all family members, including children and anyone with mobility challenges.
    - **Kid-Friendly Zones:** If you have kids, dedicate low-access storage or play zones for their use.
10. **Emotional Appeal**
    - **Inviting Atmosphere:** Incorporate scents, like candles or diffusers, and music to add to the ambiance.
    - **Minimal Stress:** Organize in a way that feels manageable and not overwhelming, even if it's not perfect.

Practical Example: A Functional Living Room

- **Purpose:** Relaxing and entertaining.
- **Declutter:** Remove unused decor, and organize remotes in a basket.
- **Storage:** Use an ottoman with storage to hide blankets and magazines.
- **Layout:** Arrange seating around a central coffee table to encourage conversation.
- **Lighting:** Add a floor lamp for reading and soft table lamps for ambiance.
- **Personal Touches:** Display a few family photos and a favorite vase.

By focusing on these aspects, you can transform your home into a space that is both functional and inviting, making daily life more enjoyable and efficient.

Interactive Element: Room Assessment Checklist

Complete your **Room-By-Room Inventory Checklist** . Start with one room and list all the problem areas. Note underutilized spaces and brainstorm potential solutions. Take a photo of the room before you start so that you can track your progress. As you make changes, document them with updated photos. This checklist and visual record will help you to stay organized and motivated.

3.2 SET REALISTIC GOALS: WHAT DOES SUCCESS LOOK LIKE FOR YOU?

When you think about organizing your space, what does success look like for you? It's important to start by defining your personal organizational goals. These goals should resonate with your everyday life, and reflect on what you truly want to achieve. Set goals that are specific, measurable, achievable, and timely. For instance: instead of a vague goal like, "organize the house," try something more specific, such as "declutter the kitchen by organizing cabinets and donating unused items by the end of the month." By breaking down your ambitions into manageable steps, and creating a dead-line, you can tackle each area with precision and purpose.

Short-term and long-term goals each play distinct roles in organizing. Short-term goals offer immediate gratification and motivation. They're the small victories that keep momentum going. I suggest using my **Daily 3: Prioritized Goals** sheet for daily goals. This focuses on the top three goals of each day so that you prioritize getting these done first. Long-term goals, while more challenging due to their scope, provide a bigger picture of what you aim to accomplish. To maintain focus, break long-term goals into smaller, actionable sub-goals. This strategy not only makes them less daunting, but it also can ensure consistent progress. By regularly reviewing and adjusting your goals, you can adapt to any changes in your circumstances, while maintaining alignment with your current priorities and resources.

Flexibility is a cornerstone of effective goal setting. Life is unpredictable, and your goals should have the elasticity to adapt as needed. Periodic goal reviews allow you to assess your progress and make necessary adjustments. Perhaps you'll discover that a goal no longer aligns with your evolving priorities, or you might identify new opportunities that warrant a shift in focus. This adaptability ensures that your organizing plan remains relevant and effective, rather than rigid and constraining. Embracing change with an open mind will help you maintain momentum and motivation, even when faced with unexpected challenges.

To track your progress and stay motivated, employ tools like the <u>GOAL TRACKING SHEET</u> in the Bonus section of the book. These visual aids provide a clear overview of your achievements, helping you celebrate milestones along the way. Milestone celebrations are crucial! Honor your efforts to reinforce the positive habits that you are cultivating. Whether it's a small reward for completing a week's worth of organizational tasks, or a more significant treat when you hit a major milestone, these celebrations provide a sense of accomplishment, encouraging continued progress. They can remind you that every step forward, no matter how small, contributes to your larger vision of a clutter-free and organized life.

Interactive Element:

Complete your **<u>GOAL TRACKING SHEET</u> *and* <u>Daily 3: Prioritized Goal sheet.</u>**

3.3 CUSTOMIZE YOUR ORGANIZING PLAN: ONE SIZE DOES NOT FIT ALL

Once you have identified your clutter personality type, use that to create a customized plan tailored to your specific needs and preferences, acknowledging the uniqueness of your situation, and providing solutions that truly fit. Use your **Room-By-Room Assessment Checklist** and **Goal Tracking Sheet** to create a **Vision Board**. A **Vision Board** can help you map out your personal nuances, offering a structured, yet flexible approach to organization. These worksheets encourage you to analyze your daily routines, preferences, and the dynamics of your household, ensuring that the organizational choices you make are not only effective, but also, sustainable. Please don't feel like it's required to create a Vision Board. Only do this extra step if you are visually motivated and would enjoy the creative outlet. I have listed step-by-step instructions as part of the bonus at the end of this book.

It's essential to take a moment to identify your unique needs and preferences. Consider your lifestyle. Do you thrive in a minimalist environment, or do you prefer a space filled with personal touches and memories? Assessing how you live, and how you interact with your space, can guide your organizational strategies. Family dynamics can also play a critical role. If you share your home with others, their habits and preferences might influence how you organize. A family with young children will have different needs than a household of adults. Self-reflection allows you to tailor organizational methods that align with your individual circumstances, creating a harmonious environment that can work for everyone involved.

Flexibility is the cornerstone of any successful organizing system. Life is dynamic, and your organizational plan should be too. Adaptable systems can accommodate various lifestyles and changes, whether it's a new job, a growing family, or a simple shifting of interests. Modular storage solutions offer a perfect example of this flexibility. These systems can be easily reconfigured, or expanded, as your needs evolve, providing a versatile solution that can grow with you. Adjustable routines can also play a key role. They can allow you to modify your organizing habits to suit changing schedules or priorities, ensuring that your plan remains relevant and effective over time.

To inspire and guide your personalization efforts, consider exploring different organizing methods. For those who embrace simplicity, a capsule wardrobe might be the ideal solution. This approach involves curating a collection of essential clothing pieces that can be mixed and matched, reducing decision fatigue, and streamlining your daily routine. On the other hand, if you are someone who values creativity and variety, creative storage methods can transform your space. Think outside the box. Use unique containers to display collections, or repurpose items like vintage suitcases, for stylish storage. These strategies will not only enhance functionality, but can also infuse your space with personality and character.

Visual Element: Personalize Your Plan

Consider creating a personalized **Vision Board** for your organizational plan. Gather images, quotes, and items that reflect your lifestyle, preferences, and goals. Arrange them on a board, or digitally, to serve as a visual guide and inspiration for your organizing journey. This exercise will help you maintain focus and motivation to ensure that your plan aligns with your personal vision.

4

MASTER TIME MANAGEMENT AND PRIORITIZATION

Have you ever found yourself rushing out the door, only to realize that you're late once again? You might have checked the clock ten times, yet somehow time slipped away unnoticed. This phenomenon, often referred to as time blindness, is a common challenge for those with ADHD. It's more than just losing track of time, it's a fundamental difficulty in perceiving how time passes, which can wreak havoc on your daily life. Tasks that seem to take minutes can stretch into hours, while important appointments and deadlines are easily overlooked. The structure of the ADHD brain alters time perception, making planning and task completion a daunting endeavor. You start a task, fully intending to finish it, but before you know it, the day has slipped past, leaving you with unfinished plans and mounting frustration.

4.1 TIME BLINDNESS

Time blindness can lead to missed appointments and deadlines, causing stress and anxiety as you scramble to catch up. You might find yourself struggling to estimate how long a task will take, often underestimating the time required and overcommitting as a result. These misjudgments can disrupt your schedule and leave you feeling overwhelmed. Understanding time blindness is the first step in regaining control. Recognizing that this is a common challenge for those with ADHD can help you approach time management with compassion and strategy.

Fortunately, there are practical strategies to mitigate the effects of time blindness. Visual timers and alarms are invaluable tools, providing external cues to keep you anchored in the present. A simple kitchen timer, or a digital app, can serve as a constant reminder of how much time has passed, and how much remains. Set alarms, not just for appointments, but also for task transitions, to ensure that you stay on track throughout the day. Periodic time checks can also enhance your awareness. Make it a habit to glance at the clock every hour, assessing your progress and adjusting your pace as needed. These techniques offer a tangible way to manage time, reducing the likelihood of slipping into the time warp that so often accompanies ADHD.

Time Blocking is another powerful method for improving focus and productivity. By allocating specific time slots for tasks, you create a structured schedule that guides your day. Start with a consistent morning routine, setting the tone for the rest of your activities. Dedicate blocks for high-focused work when you are the most alert, allowing uninterrupted time to delve into demanding tasks. This approach not only enhances concentration, but also provides a framework for your day, making it easier to navigate time-related challenges. Time blocking helps compartmentalize your tasks, reducing the overwhelm and offering a clearer path to completion.

Habit Tracking is equally important. Regular assessment can reveal patterns and areas for improvement, helping you to fine-tune your approach. Consider keeping a daily habit tracking time log, noting how you have spent each hour. This practice offers insights into productivity peaks and potential distractions. Weekly reflection sessions allow you to review your progress, identify challenges, and adjust your strategies accordingly. This ongoing evaluation fosters a deeper understanding of your time management habits, empowering you to make informed adjustments that align with your goals and needs.

Interactive Element: Personal Habit Tracking Time Audit

Take a moment to conduct a personal habit tracking time audit. For one week, keep a detailed log of how you spend your time each day. Note the duration of tasks, breaks, and any distractions. At the end of the week, review your log and identify patterns and habits. Reflect on what surprised you, and consider adjustments to improve your time management. This exercise can provide valuable insights into your habits, helping you to develop a more effective approach to mastering time management.

4.2 THE SHORT BURST TECHNIQUE

Imagine setting out to accomplish a task with a clear plan, only to find your attention wandering moments later. For many with ADHD, maintaining focus can feel like an uphill battle. This is where the Short Burst Technique comes in, offering a structured approach to work that breaks tasks into manageable intervals. Set a timer for 30 minutes of focused work followed by a 5-minute break. This cycle repeats several times, with a longer break after four sessions. The simple rhythm of work and rest helps to maintain concentration without leading to burnout. The method's predictability can be a relief, providing a clear start and finish time for each task. This approach helps to maintain motivation and accountability, particularly when distractions loom large.

These intervals might not fit everyone's needs, especially if ADHD affects your attention span or energy levels. You might find that shorter work intervals are more effective for task initiation. Instead of 30 minutes, consider starting with 10 or 15-minute periods, allowing you to ease into your work without overwhelming yourself. These shorter bursts can be particularly useful when you are tackling tasks that feel daunting, or when your motivation is low. On the other hand, longer breaks might be necessary to recharge your mental energy. Sometimes a 5-minute break doesn't quite cut it, so experiment with 10 or even 15-minute pauses to see what leaves you feeling refreshed and ready to dive back in. Finding the right balance between work and rest is the key to making the short burst technique work for you.

Experimentation with interval lengths is crucial to discovering what works best for your unique rhythm. The flexibility to adjust intervals means that you can tailor the technique to suit the demands of different tasks based upon your current energy level. Perhaps a 20-minute work session with a 10-minute break hits the sweet spot, or a 30-minute focus period followed by a leisurely 15-minute pause will suit you better. Testing different combinations can allow you to identify which setups maximize your productivity, while minimizing fatigue. The beauty of this method lies in its adaptability, ensuring that you maintain focus without feeling trapped in a rigid system. This adaptability allows the technique to evolve with your needs, accommodating the natural ebb and flow of attention and energy that ADHD often brings.

To streamline the process and keep track of your sessions, consider using Focuskeeper, Tiimo or other productivity trackers. These digital tools automate the timing of work and breaks, freeing you from the need to constantly watch the clock. They often include features like task tracking and analytics, helping you monitor your progress and identify patterns in your productivity. By using these apps, you can create a digital ally to keep you on track, providing reminders for when it's time to switch gears. This automation reduces the mental load of managing time, allowing you to direct your energy toward the work itself. The structure these apps provide helps to transform the short burst technique from a concept into a seamless part of your daily routine.

4.3 PRIORITIZATION STRATEGIES: TAKING YOU FROM CHAOS TO CLARITY

For those with ADHD, prioritizing tasks can often feel like an insurmountable challenge. The sheer volume of tasks can blur the line between what's urgent and what's important, leaving you paralyzed by indecision. Start by using a **"brain dump"** technique, where you write down all your tasks in no particular order. This helps clear your mind and creates a visual list to work from. Once you have everything written out, identify the most urgent or time-sensitive tasks and group them together. This is where prioritizing with the ABC method comes in. By assigning each task a letter: A for critical, B for important but not urgent, and C for tasks that can be postponed, you create a hierarchy that guides your daily actions. This method simplifies your decision-making and it can reduce your mental load, freeing up mental space to tackle the tasks at hand. Prioritization becomes less about juggling everything at once, and more about approaching each task methodically, with intention and purpose. By implementing these techniques, you transform an overwhelming list into a manageable, prioritized plan, bringing order to the chaos.

The **two-minute rule** is another valuable tool for prioritization. If a task takes less than two minutes to complete, do it immediately instead of putting it off. This clears small items off your list quickly and prevents them from piling up and causing stress.

You must set clear goals to effectively prioritize. Well-defined goals are maps, guiding your actions and decisions. When you know where you want to go, it becomes easier to prioritize the steps needed to get there. By breaking down larger goals into smaller, attainable tasks, you create a roadmap that directs your efforts and keeps you on track. This focus not only enhances productivity, it also fosters a sense of accomplishment as each completed task brings you closer to your desired outcome.

The journey from chaos to clarity is a dynamic process, requiring adaptability and perseverance. By incorporating these prioritization strategies, you create a framework that supports your unique needs. These methods not only tame the chaos, but they also empower you to take control of your time and energy, paving the way to a more organized and fulfilling life.

4.4 DIVIDE YOUR TASKS: BREAK DOWN THE MOUNTAIN

Imagine standing before a mountain of tasks, each one clamoring for attention and demanding urgency. It's easy for you to feel overwhelmed, especially when every task feels equally pressing. This is where dividing tasks comes in, breaking a seemingly insurmountable mountain into a series of manageable hills. By dividing tasks into smaller, more digestible parts, you gain vision and control. When you break projects into phases, you can tackle one portion at a time rather than being paralyzed by the entirety. Task division provides a clearer view, revealing the steps needed to reach your goal. It's like using a map to find your way through a dense forest. Each section that you conquer leads you closer to the clearing.

Consider a large project, such as organizing your home office. At first glance, the task might seem daunting, with papers stacked high and supplies scattered. Begin by using your **Room-By Room Inventory, Goal Tracking Sheet** and **Vision Board**. Dividing the task means you start with a drawer, then move to a shelf, and finally tackle the desk. By breaking it down into these smaller tasks, you simplify the process. Time-limited task segments also help. Allocate a set amount of time to each segment, like 15 minutes for sorting papers. This not only makes the task feel more achievable, but also instills a sense of urgency that can boost productivity. By setting limits, you prevent endless meandering, keeping your focus sharp. Each completed segment becomes a building block in your path to completion.

Maintaining motivation while working through task divisions can be challenging. Celebrating the completion of each segment can provide a motivational boost. After finishing a segment, take a moment to acknowledge your progress. This could be as simple as checking off a box on a to-do list or stepping back to admire your work. Visual progress tracking is another powerful tool. Create a visual representation of your progress by checking off the task on your **Goal Tracking Sheet**. Watching your advancement unfold visually can inspire and encourage you to keep moving forward. It turns the abstract idea of progress into something tangible and motivating. By celebrating these small victories, you maintain momentum and build confidence in your ability to tackle even larger projects.

To aid in task division, several tools can be invaluable. Trello, for example, offers digital task boards that allow you to organize tasks visually. You can create boards for each project, with cards representing individual tasks or segments. As you complete each task, move the card to a new column, providing a satisfying visual representation of progress. Sticky notes can also serve as physical reminders of your tasks. Write each task on a note and place it where you'll see it regularly. Removing a note upon completion offers a sense of accomplishment and a clear indication of progress. These tools help transform the concept of segmenting into a practical and effective strategy for managing tasks.

Task division, at its core, is about creating a roadmap through complexity. It offers a structured approach that reduces the chaos of large projects, transforming them into something manageable. By focusing on smaller, achievable parts, you maintain clarity and motivation, ensuring that you not only start, but also finish each task. This method empowers you to take control of your projects, one piece at a time, without becoming overwhelmed by the bigger picture. As you integrate task division into your routine, you'll find that tasks that once seemed daunting, become achievable, leading you to greater productivity and success.

4.5 HABIT STACKING: BUILD NEW ROUTINES ON OLD FOUNDATIONS

Imagine waking up and effortlessly transitioning from one healthy habit to another, without the struggle of remembering or forcing yourself into action. This is the magic of habit stacking, a method that links new behaviors to existing routines, creating a seamless flow in your day. Think about it like adding a new train car to an already established train line. The newly added car simply follows along, powered by the momentum of what is already in motion. By connecting a new habit to a well-established one, you can leverage the existing habit's strength to support the new one. For instance, you might pair morning stretches with brushing your teeth. As you finish your dental routine, your mind cues up the next action, stretching, without hesitation. Similarly, following breakfast with a few minutes of task planning ensures that organizing your day becomes as routine as your morning meal. This strategic pairing not only simplifies the integration of new habits, but it also reinforces the likelihood of their success.

The advantages of habit stacking are profound, primarily because they capitalize on your brain's preference for consistency and familiarity. When you attach a new behavior to a pre-existing one, the transition between activities is smoother. This connection minimizes the need for conscious effort, reducing the mental load typically required to adopt new habits. Over time, this approach increases the consistency of your routines, as each new habit is reinforced by the established one. The brain begins to associate the completion of one task with the immediate commencement of another, creating a chain reaction that boosts efficiency. This method is particularly beneficial for individuals with ADHD, as it reduces the decision fatigue that can accompany multiple daily tasks, making it easier to maintain focus and adherence.

To illustrate the power of habit stacking, consider some effective combinations that can be woven into everyday life. An evening wind-down routine might include dimming the lights after dinner, signaling your body that it's time to relax. Once the lights are low, you could engage in a brief meditation session or read a book, winding down the day with intention. These activities, linked together, create a calming sequence that prepares you for restful sleep. The simplicity of these stacked habits lies in their natural progression, each flowing into the next without abrupt transitions. By designing your stacks around existing routines, you can create a rhythm that aligns with your lifestyle, enhancing both productivity and well-being.

Creating personalized habit stacks requires a bit of introspection and creativity. Start by identifying your current routines; those anchors in your day that occur without fail. Once you've mapped these out, consider where new habits might naturally fit. Look for moments of transition, like the shift from work to home in the evening, or the start of your morning routine. These are opportunities to introduce new behaviors, building on the momentum of what you're already doing. Custom habit stack worksheets can be a useful tool in this process, helping you to visualize and plan your stacks with clarity and purpose. By taking the time to design these personalized stacks, you set yourself up for sustainable success.

4.6 CREATE A FLEXIBLE DAILY ROUTINE: FIND BALANCE

Life often feels like a whirlwind, especially when contending with the unique challenges that ADHD presents. The rigidity of a strict routine can sometimes add to the chaos rather than alleviating it. That's where the beauty of flexibility comes into play. Flexible routines are not about a complete lack of structure, but about allowing room for life's unpredictability. They accommodate changes, whether it's an unexpected meeting, a surge of energy, or a sudden dip in motivation. This adaptability is crucial, enabling you to make spontaneous adjustments without feeling like you've derailed your entire day. Embracing the natural variability in energy levels is key, as some days you might feel ready to conquer the world, while other days call for a more gentle approach. A flexible routine acknowledges these fluctuations, providing a framework that is supporting, while not confining you.

Designing a routine that suits your lifestyle begins with understanding your personal needs and preferences. It's about crafting a rhythm that feels natural and sustainable. When planning your mornings, consider what sets a positive tone for your day. Perhaps it's a quiet moment with coffee, a brief meditation, or a brisk walk. Evening routines might focus on winding down, incorporating activities that signal to your brain that it's time to relax, like reading or gentle stretching. Balancing work and leisure activities is essential, ensuring that you don't burn out from constant productivity demands. Leisure time is not a luxury; it's a necessity for maintaining overall well-being. By weaving both work and relaxation into your daily schedule, you can cultivate a more holistic approach that nourishes both mind and body.

Maintaining consistency in your routines, even when motivation wanes, requires strategic support. Routine reminders and prompts, such as alarms or calendar notifications, act as gentle nudges to keep you on track. These tools help anchor your day, especially when focus feels elusive. Habit trackers can also serve as accountability partners, offering a visual representation of your progress. By marking off completed tasks, you create a trail of accomplishment that motivates continued effort. On days when motivation is low, these tools remind you of your goals and the steps you have already taken toward achieving them. The sense of achievement that they provide can be a powerful antidote to procrastination and inertia.

Real-life examples of successful flexible routines can offer inspiration and guidance. Consider the story of Alex, a graphic designer who struggled with maintaining a consistent workflow. By implementing a routine that allowed for creative bursts and moments of rest, Alex found a balance that enhanced productivity and reduced burnout. Each day began with a morning ritual of designing inspiration boards, a task that sparked creativity. Afternoons were reserved for focused work sessions, interspersed with short breaks for physical activity. Evenings involved leisurely activities that signaled the end of the workday, helping him to maintain a clear boundary between work and personal time. This adaptable routine provided Alex with the structure needed to thrive, while honoring the natural ebb and flow of energy and creativity.

By integrating flexibility into your daily routine, you can create a system that supports you, rather than to restrict you. It's about finding a balance that allows you to be productive and present without the constant pressure of rigid schedules. This approach not only enhances your ability to manage daily tasks, but it also fosters a sense of peace and control. As you continue to refine your routines, remember that flexibility is your ally, offering the freedom to adapt and the stability to anchor your day. With these principles in mind, you can be well-equipped to create a routine that aligns with your unique rhythm and needs.

5

CONQUER CLUTTER: PHYSICAL AND DIGITAL

5.1 THE DECLUTTER BLAST: 15 MINUTES OF MOTIVATION

The clock ticks quietly in the background, and you stand at the threshold of a room overflowing with clutter. It's a scene that feels all too familiar: drawers stuffed with papers, shelves crammed with forgotten items, and each corner a testament to the chaos that has slowly crept into your life. For those with ADHD, clutter isn't just a physical inconvenience; it's a mental burden, a constant reminder of the tasks left undone. But what if there was a way to tackle this chaos in short, manageable bursts. I first heard about this method from my Mother-in-law, Gail. She was always looking for a quick way to get organized, and she loved lists! I decided to call this the declutter blast; a way to get organized quickly, offering a fresh perspective on conquering clutter without feeling overwhelmed.

A declutter blast works for all clutter personalities and is a focused, intense session of tidying up, designed to deliver quick wins and visible progress. It's about diving into the mess with purpose, while not getting lost in the details. The beauty of this method lies in its simplicity. Rather than setting aside an entire day to organize (a daunting task for anyone, let alone someone with ADHD), you dedicate a mere 15 minutes to a specific area. This could be a drawer, a section of your desk, or even a corner of your living room. The goal is to create a sense of accomplishment that fuels further action. By concentrating your efforts in short bursts, you avoid the fatigue that often sets in from prolonged decluttering sessions.

The power of a declutter blast lies in the immediate visual impact that it creates. Within minutes, you can transform a cluttered space into one of order and clarity. This quick turnaround not only enhances your environment, but it can also serve as a powerful motivator. Seeing tangible results from your efforts boosts your confidence, encouraging you to tackle other areas with renewed vigor. It's akin to watching a time-lapse video of a messy room being transformed into a tidy oasis, where each item finds its rightful place and the chaos gives way to calm. The enhanced sense of accomplishment that follows is a reward in itself, reinforcing the benefits of these focused sessions.

To conduct a successful declutter blast, start by setting a timer. This not only keeps you on track but also helps manage your time effectively. Choose a specific area to focus on, like a cluttered kitchen drawer or a pile of unopened mail. By narrowing your focus, you can prevent being overwhelmed while maintaining clarity on what needs to be done. Begin by removing everything from the chosen space, assessing each item carefully. Decide what to keep, what to donate, and what to discard. Utilize existing containers or dividers to organize the remaining items, ensuring that everything has a designated spot. As the timer counts down, maintain your momentum, knowing that in just a few minutes, you will have completed a tangible step toward order.

Incorporating declutter blasts into your weekly routine can transform organization from a daunting task into a habitual practice. Consider setting a regular schedule, perhaps dedicating 15 minutes each Saturday morning to a specific area in need of attention. This consistency not only maintains order but also prevents clutter from accumulating in the first place. Track your progress over time, noting which areas have been successfully blasted, and which ones still require your attention. This record not only provides a sense of achievement but also helps you to identify patterns and areas where clutter tends to reappear. By making declutter blasts a regular feature in your life, you cultivate a proactive approach to organization, ensuring that clutter never becomes an insurmountable challenge again.

Here's an example of what a 15 Minute Blast looks like:

1. **Set a Timer:** Start by setting a timer for 15 minutes. The time limit provides structure and reduces the feeling of overwhelm by making the task feel manageable.
2. **Choose a Small, Defined Area:** Focus on a single drawer, a countertop, or a section of a room—something small and contained. For example, decide to tackle the top of your dresser or a single kitchen drawer.
3. **Use the "Trash, Donate, Keep" Method:** Quickly sort items into three categories:
    - **Trash:** Items that are broken, expired, or unusable.
    - **Donate:** Items in good condition that you no longer need or use.
    - **Keep:** Items you actively use and need to store properly.

4. **Make Quick Decisions:** Avoid overthinking. If you hesitate, place the item in a "Maybe" pile and revisit it later.
5. **Return "Keep" Items to Their Homes:** Once sorted, immediately put the "keep" items back in their rightful places. For example, clothes go in drawers, keys go on a hook, and pens go in a pencil holder.
6. **Wrap Up with a Quick Check:** When the timer goes off, stop and admire what you've accomplished, even if it's a small dent. Celebrate the progress and remind yourself that consistent 15-minute sessions add up over time.

In just 15 minutes, you could clear a cluttered surface, sort through a drawer, or significantly reduce visual chaos in your home. Keeping the task small and focused is key to staying motivated and avoiding overwhelm.

Interactive Element: Weekly Blast Tracker

Create a simple chart to track your declutter blasts or use the one I've created for you in the Bonus section. List each week with a space to note the area tackled, and a brief reflection on the results. Use this tracker to plan future blasts, ensuring that all areas receive attention over time. This visual tool will help maintain consistency and celebrate your ongoing progress.

5.2 EMOTIONAL ATTACHMENT: LET GO WITH CONFIDENCE

Clutter isn't just about physical objects; it's about the emotional strings attached to them. For many, these items aren't just things. They are memories, moments frozen in time. A concert ticket stub might remind you of an unforgettable night. A worn-out sweater might evoke the warmth of a loved one's embrace. The sentimental value of these objects can create a powerful emotional barrier, making it difficult for you to part with them. Yet, the accumulation of such items can lead to overwhelming clutter, hindering your ability to create a space that will truly serve you. The fear of regret or loss often looms large, whispering doubts into the process of decluttering. What if I need this one day? What if letting go means losing a piece of myself? These thoughts can paralyze your efforts to declutter, trapping you in a cycle where the past continually impedes the present.

To break free from these emotional shackles, consider implementing strategies that guide you through the process.

- **Understand the Source of Attachment:** Identify the Emotion: Reflect on why the object feels significant. Is it tied to a loved one, a specific memory, or a fear of losing something important? Separate the Object from the Memory: Remind yourself that the memory or relationship is not dependent on the object itself—it exists in your mind and heart.
- **Start Small:** Choose Low-Stakes Items: Begin with items that hold less emotional weight, like unused gifts or duplicate items. One Area at a Time: Focus on a small area, such as a drawer or a shelf, to avoid feeling overwhelmed.
- **Use the "Yes-No-Maybe" Method:** Yes: Keep items you use or truly love. No: Discard or donate items you no longer need. Maybe: Place uncertain items in a box. If you don't use or miss them within six months, let them go.
- **Take Photos:** Capture an image of the item before letting it go. A photo preserves the memory while freeing up physical space.

- **Reframe Your Thinking**: Focus on the Benefits of Letting Go: Remind yourself of the space, peace, and clarity you'll gain. Consider the Object's Future Use: Imagine someone else benefiting from the item rather than it sitting unused.
- **Create a "Memory Box"**: Limit sentimental items to a single box. This boundary helps prioritize what truly matters. This box becomes a sanctuary for items of deep sentimental value, allowing you to preserve the memories without overwhelming your space. By selecting a few cherished objects to keep, you can honor the memories while still moving toward a clutter-free environment.
- **Involve Someone You Trust**: Ask a friend, family member, or accountability partner to help you evaluate items objectively. Share the story behind the item; sometimes expressing your feelings can make it easier to let go.
- **Set Clear Goals:** Decide how much space you want to reclaim or what specific areas you want to declutter. Use a timeline to prevent procrastination.
- **Honor the Object's Role:** Acknowledge the item's past significance: "Thank you for serving me." Say goodbye to the item to emotionally close the chapter.
- **Practice the "One-Year Rule"**: If you haven't used or thought about the item in a year, it's likely time to part ways. My husband has been a huge proponent of this rule for our entire married life. This rule requires you to really consider the item and it helps you to prioritize items that add value to your present, rather than those tied solely to the past.
- **Donate with Purpose:** Knowing your item will help someone else can ease guilt about letting it go. Donate to organizations that align with your values (e.g., shelters, charities).

- **Recognize the Cost of Keeping:** Consider the physical, emotional, and mental toll of holding onto clutter. Think about the energy and space you'll reclaim by letting go.
- **Replace Guilt with Gratitude:** Let go of guilt associated with discarding gifts or inherited items. Be grateful for the intent or relationship behind the object, not the item itself.
- **Envision Your Ideal Space:** Imagine what a peaceful, decluttered home looks and feels like. Use that vision as motivation to release items that don't contribute to your ideal environment.

Self-reflection and mindfulness play crucial roles in understanding your emotional responses to clutter. Journaling about your feelings toward specific items can provide clarity and insight. What memories do they evoke? Why is it difficult to let them go? By exploring these questions, you can gain a deeper understanding of the emotional ties that bind you to certain objects. Mindful meditation can also ease the anxiety associated with decluttering. Take a few minutes to breathe deeply, centering yourself in the present moment. This practice can help calm your mind, making it easier for you to approach decluttering with a sense of peace and patience. By cultivating awareness, you can transform decluttering from a daunting task into an opportunity for personal growth and self-discovery.

Letting go of unnecessary items can lead to profound benefits, both mentally and physically. As you release objects that no longer serve you, you create space for mental clarity to emerge. The weight of excessive belongings lifts, freeing your mind to focus on what truly matters. This newfound clarity reduces stress and enhances your ability to navigate daily life with intention and purpose. Moreover, an organized living space improves functionality. When each item has a designated place, your environment becomes more efficient and supportive of your lifestyle. You spend less time searching for things and more time engaging in activities that bring joy and fulfillment. Embracing the process of letting go not only transforms your physical surroundings, but it also nurtures a sense of freedom and empowerment, allowing you to shape a life that aligns with your values and aspirations.

5.3 SIMPLIFY SPACES: PRACTICAL TIPS FOR EVERY ROOM

Kitchen:

The kitchen might be a place where you find a mishmash of gadgets and utensils, some of which haven't seen the light of day in months. This common clutter zone can be tamed using these effective tactics.

1. **Pare down to the essentials:** Begin by assessing which tools you genuinely use. Do you really need three different peelers? Do you use that Panini press more than once per year? Focus on the gadgets and utensils that serve multiple functions. A sharp chef's knife might replace a clutter of specialized slicers.
2. **Tackle one category at a time:** Utensils, cookware, or pantry items, rather than trying to do the entire kitchen at once. Streamlining your kitchen is about creating a space where cooking feels less like a chore, and more like a creative enterprise.
3. **Neat countertops:** Only keep daily-use appliances (like a coffee maker or toaster) on the counter. Store everything else in cabinets to keep surfaces clear and visually calming. The space not only looks better, but also provides a

functional workspace where you can prepare meals without constantly shifting things around.
4. **Drawer Dividers:** Imagine opening a drawer where each tool has its own spot, is easy to find, and even easier to put back after its use. I use the expandable bamboo drawer dividers I found on Amazon. You can also find drawer inserts but most of them are standard drawer size and lack malleability. I like the bamboo inserts because they are expandable and moveable to fit different sized items and drawer sizes.
5. **One-Year Rule:** Remove items you're holding onto for "someday". If you haven't used them in the past year, put them in the trash or donate bin. This might include niche gadgets like an avocado slicer.
6. **Establish a "One-In-One-Out" Rule:** For every new item you bring into the kitchen, remove an old one. This helps maintain balance and prevents clutter from accumulating.

Pantry:

The pantry can be another hot spot for clutter and disorganization.

1. **Start by Emptying the Pantry:** Take everything out to get a clear view of what you have. This makes it easier to assess what's expired, unused, or unnecessary. Wipe down shelves and bins to start with a clean slate. Sort by keep, expired (throw away) and donate.
2. **Check Expiration Dates:** Discard expired items and stale products. If you find unopened items that are still good but you won't use, consider donating them to a food pantry.
3. **Group Items by Category:** Organize food into categories like canned goods, snacks, baking supplies, grains, and

spices. Use labeled bins or baskets to keep similar items together and make them easy to find.

4. **Use Clear Containers:** Transfer dry goods (like flour, sugar, pasta, and cereal) into clear, airtight containers. This keeps food fresh, saves space, and makes it easy to see what you have. For other items, use clear open-top bins and clearly label each bin. The shape of the bin is important so that you don't lose space with mismatched containers that don't fit together. Boxed items such as rice mixes, cake mixes, etc., can be contained in a clear bin. Wal-mart has a great selection of these clear bins. They are inexpensive and fit together neatly.

5. **Utilize Vertical Space:** Add shelf risers, stackable bins, or hanging organizers to maximize vertical storage space. Use the back of the pantry door for hanging spice racks or storage for small items like spice packets.

6. **Keep Frequently Used Items Accessible:** Place everyday essentials like snacks, cooking oils, or breakfast foods at eye level. Store less-used or seasonal items (e.g., holiday baking supplies) on higher or lower shelves.

7. **Establish a Rotation System:** Practice "first in, first out" (FIFO) by placing newer items behind older ones. This ensures food gets used before it expires and reduces waste.

8. **Grocery List:** The pantry is also a great place for a Grocery List. This can be a whiteboard, a paper list, a computerized list maker, etc. How you keep a visual list is not important. The location and ease of use is important. If the list is not in a place where you can see it, you will not remember to use it. A stocked pantry that is organized and clearly labeled is calming and makes cooking more efficient.

Linen Closet:

Consider the benefits of a streamlined linen closet.

1. **Purge Unnecessary Items:** Eliminate Worn-Out Linens: Discard towels, sheets, or blankets that are ripped, stained, or no longer used. Keep only the towels, blankets, and linens that you actually use, organizing them by color, folding them neatly, or rolling them to save space. Stick to a Practical Inventory: Keep no more than 2-3 sets of sheets and towels per person or bed. Donate excess items to shelters or animal rescues.
2. **Organize by Category:** Group items into categories such as sheets, towels, blankets, and table linens. Use labeled bins or shelf dividers to keep similar items together and prevent them from mixing. Store sheet sets together in one of its pillowcases, then label it with King, Queen, Full, or Twin. This makes linen changes quick and efficient.
3. **Fold Linens Neatly:** Use uniform folding techniques to maximize space and maintain a tidy appearance. Store sheets in their matching pillowcases to keep sets together and easy to grab.
4. **Use Vertical Storage Solutions:** Add stackable bins, baskets, or shelf risers to make use of vertical space. Use over-the-door organizers for smaller items like washcloths or pillowcases.
5. **Keep Frequently Used Items Accessible:** Place everyday essentials, like bath towels and current-season bedding, at eye level for easy access. Store less-used or seasonal items, like beach towels or holiday tablecloths, on higher or lower shelves.

Bedroom:

The Bedroom is another area that can become cluttered. Organizing your bedroom starts with creating a calm and functional space.

1. **Declutter Surfaces:** Nightstands and dressers often collect random items, so keep them clear by designating a small tray or box for essentials like a book, glasses, or a phone charger. Store everything else out of sight in drawers or bins to maintain a clean look.
2. **Closet organization:** This is the key to an orderly bedroom. Arrange clothing by type and season, and consider investing in slim, matching hangers to maximize space. Use bins or baskets for accessories like scarves and belts, and keep shoes organized on racks or shelves to avoid piles on the floor. If your closet space is limited, under-bed storage can be a lifesaver for off-season clothes or spare linens.
3. **Laundry:** Create a system for handling laundry to prevent piles from accumulating. Use separate hampers for darks, lights, and delicates to simplify sorting. Make it a habit to fold and put away clean laundry immediately rather than letting it linger in baskets. Try to stack this with another habit you already have.
4. **Create a Beautiful and Neat bed:** Your bed is the focal point of the room, so keep it inviting and organized. Use a simple, clean bedding setup and store extra pillows and blankets in a storage ottoman or under-bed bin to keep them accessible but out of the way. Keeping the bed made daily can set a positive tone for the room - again consider habit stacking. First brush your teeth, then make your bed.

Bathroom:

Bathrooms are generally a tight space that benefits from minimalism.

1. **Clean Countertops:** Organizing your bathroom begins with decluttering the countertops to create a clean and serene environment. Keep only the essentials, like soap, toothbrushes, or lotion, on the counter and store everything else in drawers or cabinets.
2. **Group Similar Items:** Use trays or small organizers to group similar items, making it easier to maintain order and quickly find what you need.
3. **Dividers and bins are essential:** Inside cabinets and drawers, maximize space with dividers, bins, or stackable containers. Group items by category, such as haircare, skincare, and first aid, and label the containers for clarity.
4. **Under-sink storage:** UFor under-sink storage, consider tiered shelves or pull-out organizers to make use of vertical space and prevent items from getting lost in the back.
5. **Towel Storage:** Towel storage is essential in a functional bathroom. If you're tight on space, install hooks on the walls or back of the door for hanging towels, and use a small basket or shelf for rolled spare towels. For a streamlined look, limit the number of towels and rotate them regularly.
6. **Caddy or Wall-mounted Organizers:** In the shower or tub area, avoid clutter by using a caddy or wall-mounted organizer to keep shampoo, conditioner, and soap neatly contained. Choose products with pump dispensers or refillable containers to reduce the visual noise of mismatched bottles.

7. **Restocking and Maintenance:** Finally, incorporate a system for restocking and maintenance. Store backup supplies like toilet paper, toothpaste, and cleaning products in an easily accessible location. Regularly declutter expired or unused items to prevent buildup. By creating designated spaces for everything and staying on top of maintenance, your bathroom will remain an organized and stress-free space.

An organized bathroom not only speeds up your morning routine, but it can also set a calming tone for the day. Picture reaching for your toothbrush without knocking over a precarious tower of products. This ease of use is key to maintaining a clutter-free environment that serves you efficiently.

Whole Home Tips:

1. **Function vs. Aesthetics:** The pursuit of simplicity often leads to a revelation; functionality trumps aesthetics. While a perfectly curated Instagram-worthy space might seem appealing, the reality is that practicality is what makes your home truly livable.
2. **Transparency:** Accessible storage solutions, such as open shelving or clear bins, allow you to see what you have at a glance. This transparency reduces the time spent searching for items, making everyday tasks more straightforward.
3. **Multi-functionality:** Multi-functional furniture, like a coffee table with built-in storage, can perform double duty, providing both style and utility. The goal is not to sacrifice beauty, but to integrate it seamlessly with function, creating a home that is both welcoming and workable.
4. **Simplicity:** Maintaining simplicity over time requires commitment and routine. Regularly scheduled

decluttering checks can prevent the slow creep of clutter. Set aside time each month to assess your space using your **Room-to-Room Checklist**, removing items that no longer serve you.
5. **Seasonal Rotation:** Store away winter coats during the summer months, and bring them back out as the temperature drops. This practice not only keeps your wardrobe fresh but also frees up valuable space for other essentials.

By making decluttering a regular habit, you can ensure that your home remains a place of order and tranquility, and free from the stress of excess.

5.4 DIGITAL DECLUTTERING: ORGANIZE YOUR VIRTUAL LIFE

In today's digital age, clutter isn't confined to our physical spaces. It extends into our virtual lives, often with greater consequences. Overloaded email inboxes and disorganized digital files can silently wreak havoc on your productivity and increase your stress levels, creating a sense of chaos that's hard to escape. Picture the frustration of sifting through hundreds of emails to find that one important message, or spending precious minutes searching for a file that you know you saved somewhere. These digital disarray moments can stall your day, making even simple tasks feel overwhelming. Recognizing the impact of digital clutter is the first step toward regaining control and fostering an organized digital environment that supports rather than hindering your daily activities.

To address this virtual chaos, adopting strategies for decluttering digital spaces is crucial. A popular technique is achieving "Inbox Zero," a method that encourages maintaining an empty or near-empty email inbox. Start by sorting emails into folders based on urgency and relevance, ensuring that only critical items remain in your main inbox. Use tools like filters and rules to automatically categorize incoming emails. This can help you to manage the influx without feeling buried. Similarly, using a consistent file naming strategy can streamline file organization. Create a consistent system that categorizes files by type or project, reducing the time spent searching for documents. For example: if you are working on Real Estate files, you could start the file names with the customer name, followed by the street name, and then the document type. IE: Miller Longview Title or Miller Longview 35E. This approach not only declutters your virtual space, it also enhances efficiency and focus, allowing you to navigate your digital world with ease and confidence.

Digital tools can play a pivotal role in maintaining an organized virtual life. Cloud storage solutions like Google Drive, Microsoft Onedrive, or Dropbox offer a centralized location for files, accessible from any device, reducing the need for physical storage and the risk of losing important documents. Task management tools such as Evernote allow for seamless organization of notes, ideas, and to-do lists, providing a digital workspace where everything you need is at your fingertips. These tools help automate organization, taking the burden off your memory and ensuring that important information is always within reach. By incorporating these digital aids, you can create a supportive infrastructure that simplifies your digital interactions while reducing the cognitive load associated with managing multiple tasks and data.

Regular digital maintenance practices are essential to prevent the accumulation of digital clutter over time. Consider conducting monthly digital file audits, where you evaluate your stored files and delete those that are outdated or unnecessary. This practice not only frees up storage space but also keeps your digital workspace clean and efficient. Weekly email organization sessions can further support this effort, providing a dedicated time to sort through new messages, address pending items, and maintain the order achieved with Inbox Zero. By incorporating these routines into your schedule, you establish a habit of digital tidiness to ensure that clutter never becomes an insurmountable problem again. This proactive approach fosters a digital environment that is conducive to your productivity and to your well-being.

Efficient digital organization is more than just a convenience; it is a gateway to enhanced productivity and reduced stress. With a clear and structured digital space, you can focus on what truly matters without the constant distraction of virtual clutter. The strategies outlined here are designed to empower you to take charge of your digital life, creating a virtual environment that supports your goals and aspirations. By embracing these practices, you pave the way for a more organized, harmonious life both online and offline.

5.5 STREAMLINED SYSTEMS: REDUCE EFFORT TO MAINTAIN ORDER

Imagine walking into your home and everything has its place, without the usual hassle of figuring out where to put things. This is the magic of a streamlined system: an approach that simplifies your daily routines by minimizing the effort needed to keep your space organized. It's about creating an environment where organization becomes second nature, rather than a task that you dread. By reducing the barriers to maintaining order, these systems make it easier to stay consistent and prevent clutter from taking over. Consider your entryway, for instance. A streamlined solution might include a small table with a bowl for keys and a few hooks for bags, coats, and an organizer for your shoes. This setup ensures that as soon as you step inside, you have a designated spot to drop your essentials. Not only does this keep the entryway tidy, but it also reduces the time spent searching for misplaced items when you're in a hurry to leave.

Simple, intuitive systems, like open shelving, can further enhance the ease of access to everyday items. In the pantry, for example: clear containers allow you to see what you have at a glance, making meal prep more efficient and less stressful. When everything is visible and within reach, you are less likely to buy duplicates or forget about ingredients that you already own. This transparency helps maintain a clutter-free kitchen, where each item has a purpose and a place. These systems aren't just about tidiness; they are about creating a harmonious space that supports your lifestyle. Quick retrieval and replacement of items become effortless, reducing the mental load of organization, allowing you to focus on more important aspects of your day.

Streamlined systems are not one-size-fits-all; they thrive on customization to meet individual needs. Tailoring these systems to fit your personal preferences and the dynamics of your household can make a significant difference in their effectiveness. Maybe you live with multiple family members, each with their own set of keys and bags. Personalized hooks labeled with each person's name can prevent mix-ups, ensuring that everyone knows where to find their belongings. Similarly, if you have young children, consider creating a low shelf for their shoes and backpacks, encouraging them to take responsibility for their own items. By adapting these systems to your unique situation, you can create an environment that not only stays organized, but it also teaches valuable habits to everyone in the household.

The beauty of streamlined systems lies in their adaptability and simplicity, making them accessible to everyone, regardless of their organizing prowess. They transform the act of tidying up from a chore, into an automatic behavior, seamlessly integrated into your daily routine. As you embrace these systems, you'll find that the time and energy once spent on managing clutter can now be redirected toward more fulfilling pursuits. This shift not only enhances your productivity, but it also contributes to a more peaceful and enjoyable living space, where order is maintained without the constant struggle.

5.6 SUSTAINABLE DECLUTTERING HABITS: KEEP SPACES CLEAR

In the whirlwind of daily life, it's easy to let clutter creep back in, subtly reclaiming corners of your home and mind. The key to maintaining a clutter-free environment lies in developing sustainable habits that prioritize long-term maintenance, over temporary fixes. Imagine starting your day with a 15 minute declutter blast tidying routine: a small ritual that sets the tone for order and clarity. Whether it's making your bed, clearing your desk, or putting away dishes, these daily acts form the backbone of a tidy space. They must become automatic, requiring little mental effort, while providing a significant impact on your environment. The effect of these routines is cumulative, creating a foundation that supports a clutter-free lifestyle.

Mindful purchasing practices are another pillar of sustainability. Before bringing a new item into your home, pause to consider its necessity. Will it add value, or will it become yet another thing to manage? This approach helps curb impulsive buying, a common challenge for many with ADHD. By thoughtfully evaluating purchases, you can prevent clutter from accumulating in the first place. It also saves you from the cycle of decluttering and reaccumulation, a frustrating pattern that can undermine your efforts.

Integrating decluttering into your daily life doesn't have to be a monumental task. It can be as simple as using commercial breaks during a TV show to tidy up a room, or using transitions between tasks as opportunities to organize. These small windows of time add up, transforming clutter management into a regular habit, rather than a sporadic event. By embedding decluttering into these natural pauses, you can create a rhythm that keeps your environment in check without overwhelming yourself.

The benefits of sustained decluttering efforts extend beyond mere aesthetics. A clear, organized space reduces stress and anxiety, creating an environment that supports mental well-being. The visual calm of a tidy room can have a profound effect on your mood, enhancing your sense of control and peace. Additionally, an organized space boosts productivity and focus. When your surroundings are in order, your mind is free to concentrate on the tasks at hand without the distraction of chaos. This clarity can allow you to be more efficient, making it easier to accomplish your goals and enjoy the activities you love.

As you continue to cultivate these sustainable habits, you'll discover that maintaining a clutter-free space becomes second nature. The initial effort to establish these routines pays off in the long run, providing a foundation for a more organized, fulfilling life. Each small action contributes to a larger picture, shaping an environment that reflects and supports your values and aspirations.

5.7 VISUAL ORGANIZATION: USE COLOR AND DESIGN TO ENHANCE ORDER

Have you ever walked into a space and felt an immediate sense of clarity and calm, simply because it was visually organized? Color and design play pivotal roles in achieving such serenity. They transform spaces into intuitive environments where everything is both aesthetically pleasing, and easy to find. Color-coded filing systems are a prime example of this. By assigning specific colors to different categories of documents, you can instantly identify what you need. Imagine opening a file drawer and seeing a rainbow of folders, each hue representing a distinct aspect of your life: bills in blue, medical records in red, and personal documents in green. This system reduces the time spent searching through piles and helps to keep your mind at ease.

Designated zones marked with color can further streamline your space. Using color markers to delineate areas for different activities or items is a simple yet effective strategy. In a shared office, for instance, a green-taped section of the table could signify a communal supply area, while a yellow one designating personal workspace. This visual clarity minimizes confusion to ensure that everyone knows where things belong. It can turn chaotic spaces into well-organized zones that support productivity and harmony.

Implementing visual organization requires some creativity, but it also offers immense benefits. Labeling with colorful tags is a straightforward way to identify contents without needing to open drawers or boxes. These tags can be as simple as sticky notes or as elaborate as printed labels. Meanwhile, design patterns can denote categories, adding an extra layer of organization. Consider using patterned washi tape to wrap around cables, with each pattern representing a different device or function. This not only prevents tangling but also speeds up the process of finding the right cable in a drawer full of them. Such visual cues make retrieving and replacing items a breeze, turning organization from a chore into a seamless part of your routine.

Visual cues significantly impact habit formation by facilitating routine adherence and consistency. A calendar with color-coded tasks can serve as a daily reminder of what's on your plate, helping you to stay on track. Visual reminders for daily tasks, such as sticky notes on the bathroom mirror, or brightly colored magnets on the fridge, can ensure that important chores are never forgotten. These small, consistent signals reinforce habits over time, embedding them into your daily life. Your brain responds well to visual stimuli, making it easier to remember and complete tasks without relying solely on memory.

Real-world examples abound of the transformative power of visual organization. Take a workspace, where bright colors distinguish between files, supplies, and personal items. Such a setup not only boosts efficiency but also makes the environment more inviting and stimulating. Similarly, an organized closet with color-coded sections can allow for quick outfit selection, streamlining your morning routine. By arranging clothes by color or type, you can create an orderly space that not only looks good, but also saves time. These examples highlight the practical benefits of visual organization, demonstrating how thoughtful design can enhance clarity and function in everyday life.

As we wrap up this chapter, consider how these principles of visual organization can be woven into your space. By embracing color and design, you can create an environment that not only looks orderly, but also supports your lifestyle. This chapter has laid the foundation for a clutter-free life, both physically and digitally. Up next, we'll explore how this newfound order can boost productivity and reduce stress, paving the way for a more efficient and serene existence.

6

ENHANCE PRODUCTIVITY AND REDUCE STRESS

6.1 OPTIMIZE YOUR WORKSPACE

You sit down at your desk, ready to tackle the tasks ahead. The environment around you plays a huge role in how effectively you can focus and manage your day. A well-organized workspace isn't just about aesthetics; it's about functionality and productivity. When your space supports your efforts, you can find it easier to concentrate and accomplish your goals.

A productive environment begins with an ergonomic desk setup. Imagine a desk that adjusts to your height, allowing you to switch between sitting and standing. This simple feature can transform your workspace into a comfortable haven, reducing physical strain and enhancing focus. An ergonomic chair complements this setup, providing the necessary support to prevent back and shoulder pain. By maintaining physical comfort, you can give more attention to your tasks, minimizing distractions caused by discomfort. A clutter-free work surface is equally important. Clear away unnecessary items, leaving only what you need to do the job at hand. This decluttered space can reduce visual distractions to foster a sense of calm, allowing you to concentrate fully on your next task.

Optimizing the spatial layout of your workspace can further enhance productivity. Consider the strategic placement of your furniture. Position your desk to face a window, if possible, allowing natural light to illuminate your work area. This not only boosts your mood but also reduces eye strain. Ensure that pathways within your space are clear and unobstructed. This promotes easy movement and can prevent the frustration of navigating around obstacles. A well-planned layout facilitates efficient workflow, enabling you to move seamlessly from one task to another without unnecessary interruptions. The arrangement of your workspace should reflect the flow of your work, with frequently used items within arm's reach and less essential items stored neatly away.

Lighting and ambiance play crucial roles in influencing productivity. Natural light is a powerful ally, but it's not always available. Incorporate task lighting to brighten your workspace when needed. The right balance of warm and cool tones can enhance cognitive ability and focus, creating an environment conducive to concentration. In addition to lighting, consider the color palette of your workspace. Calming colors, such as soft blues or greens, can create a soothing atmosphere, reducing stress and promoting mental clarity. Your workspace should be a sanctuary, a place where you feel relaxed, yet focused, ready to tackle whatever challenges the day brings.

Maintaining a productive environment requires consistent effort and attention. Implement end-of-day reset rituals to leave your workspace ready for the next day. Take a few minutes to tidy up, file away papers, and organize your desk. This simple habit sets a positive tone for the next work session, allowing you to start fresh without the burden of yesterday's clutter. Establish regular cleaning schedules to keep your space organized, and free of dust and debris. These routines not only maintain the physical environment, but they also reinforce a mindset of organization and discipline. When your workspace is in order, your mind is free to focus on what truly matters.

Interactive Element: Workspace Reflection Exercise

Take a moment to reflect on your current workspace. What elements support your productivity, and what could be improved? Consider the layout, lighting, and overall ambiance. Make a list of changes you'd like to implement, whether it's rearranging furniture or introducing new lighting. Document your reflections and plan for adjustments that will transform your workspace into a hub of focus and efficiency.

6.2 OVERCOME PROCRASTINATION: PRACTICAL TIPS FOR ACTION

Picture this: you sit down to start a task, but hours slip by as you struggle to begin. This cycle of procrastination is a common hurdle, especially when ADHD is in the mix. Understanding why you procrastinate is key to breaking the cycle. Often, it's the fear of failure, or the pressure of perfectionism that holds you back. You worry about not meeting expectations, so you delay starting. This fear can paralyze you, making tasks seem insurmountable. The size of the task itself can also overwhelm you, leaving you unsure of where to begin. When a project looms large, it's easy to let procrastination take over, while you convince yourself that you'll start "tomorrow."

To combat procrastination, try breaking tasks into smaller, manageable steps. Instead of tackling an entire project at once, divide it into bite-sized pieces. This approach makes the task less intimidating and allows you to focus on one step at a time. Setting specific, achievable deadlines for each step can further enhance this strategy. Having a clear timeline can provide structure and accountability, encouraging you to make steady progress. You might find it helpful to write down these deadlines and check off tasks as you complete them. This visual representation of progress can boost motivation and provide a sense of accomplishment.

Accountability plays a significant role in overcoming procrastination. Partnering with an accountability buddy can be a game-changer. Share your goals with someone who understands your challenges and can offer support. This partnership creates a sense of shared responsibility, making it harder to put off tasks. Knowing someone else is counting on you can be a powerful motivator. Regular check-ins with your buddy can provide encouragement and keep you on track, ensuring that you stay committed to your goals. The mutual support and understanding fostered in this relationship can transform procrastination into productivity.

Motivational triggers can also help you initiate action and stay on course. Consider implementing a reward system for task completion. Promise yourself a small treat or break once you finish a task. These rewards don't have to be extravagant, but they should be meaningful to you. Whether it's enjoying your favorite snack, taking a walk, or watching an episode of a beloved show, these incentives provide a tangible goal to work toward. By associating tasks with positive outcomes, you can create a cycle of motivation and achievement. This approach turns work into a series of opportunities for reward, making the process more enjoyable and less daunting.

Procrastination can feel like a familiar foe, but it doesn't have to dictate your actions. By understanding its roots and implementing strategies to overcome it, you can take control of your time and productivity. Breaking tasks into smaller steps, setting deadlines, seeking accountability, and using motivational triggers, can transform how you approach your to-do list. As you incorporate these strategies, you'll likely find that tasks become less overwhelming and more manageable. The shift from procrastination to productivity isn't about perfection; it's about progress, one small step at a time.

6.3 BALANCE AESTHETICS AND FUNCTIONALITY: PRACTICAL OVER PERFECTION

In the realm of organization, practicality is paramount. The seductive allure of a beautifully styled room can sometimes overshadow its functionality. However, when you prioritize practical solutions, the benefits are tangible and enduring. Efficient storage solutions are a cornerstone of this approach. Imagine a closet where every item has its place, from neatly folded linens to accessible everyday wear. The goal is to create an environment where reaching for what you need is effortless, reducing the frustration of searching through disorganized piles. Accessible setups mean placing frequently used items within easy reach, eliminating unnecessary steps and keeping your daily routines smooth and efficient. This focus on functionality ensures that your space serves you, making day-to-day living more manageable and less stressful.

Finding a balance between aesthetics and usability doesn't mean sacrificing one for the other. It's about creating spaces that are both visually appealing and practical. Dual-purpose furniture is a brilliant example of this balance. Consider a coffee table that doubles as a storage unit, or an ottoman with a hidden compartment. These pieces provide the elegance and utility you need to maximize space without cluttering it. Similarly, selecting harmonious color schemes can enhance organization. Soft neutral tones create a calming backdrop, allowing your organizational systems to shine. By choosing colors that complement your decor, you maintain visual cohesion, making your space feel both inviting and orderly. This thoughtful integration of aesthetics and practicality transforms your environment, ensuring that it reflects your personal style while supporting your organizational goals.

Personal expression within organizing is not just an option; it's a necessity for creating spaces that resonate with you. Displaying meaningful items can infuse your environment with character and warmth. Perhaps it's a collection of travel souvenirs, or family photographs. These elements tell your story, making your space uniquely yours. However, it's important to strike a balance so that personal touches enhance, rather than overwhelm. Grouping similar items together can create a cohesive display that adds to the room's aesthetic without detracting from its functionality. The key is to showcase pieces that inspire you, bringing joy and motivation into your daily life. By incorporating personal style into practical organizing, you can create a home that is not only functional, but also a true reflection of your identity.

Maintaining a balance over time requires regular reassessment of your space needs. As life evolves, so do the demands on your environment. Periodically evaluate your setup, considering whether it still meets your current needs, or if adjustments are necessary. Perhaps a new hobby requires additional storage, or a change in lifestyle warrants a different furniture arrangement. By staying attuned to these shifts, you ensure that your space continues to serve you effectively. This ongoing process of evaluation and adaptation keeps your environment dynamic and responsive, allowing it to grow and change with you. Regular reassessment prevents stagnation, ensuring that your space remains both beautiful and functional, and always aligned with your evolving life.

6.4 USE TECHNOLOGY TO STAY ORGANIZED: APPS AND TOOLS FOR ADHD

In today's digital age, technology offers a wealth of tools designed to support organization, especially for those navigating the complexities of ADHD. Imagine having a digital assistant at your fingertips, ready to streamline tasks and keep you on track. Task management apps like Todoist are invaluable for capturing and organizing tasks. They allow you to create detailed lists, set priorities, and even delegate tasks if needed. The beauty of digital tools lies in their ability to adapt to your rhythm, providing reminders and notifications that gently nudge you back on course. These alerts act as external cues, helping you to manage time more effectively to reduce the chances of tasks slipping through the cracks.

Digital note-taking tools like Evernote provide a versatile platform for managing information. Whether you're jotting down a fleeting thought or organizing detailed project notes, Evernote offers a centralized space to store and sort your ideas. Its robust search functionality means that you can easily retrieve information, even amidst a sea of notes. Visual task tracking boards, such as those offered by Trello, cater to the ADHD mind by providing a clear, visual representation of tasks. These boards break projects into manageable segments, allowing you to see progress at a glance. By moving tasks from 'To Do' to 'Done,' you gain a tangible sense of accomplishment, motivating continued productivity.

Integrating technology into your daily routines can be a game-changer. Start by syncing calendars across devices, ensuring that you have access to your schedule wherever you are. This integration prevents double-booking and keeps you aware of upcoming commitments. Consider setting aside a few minutes each morning to review your digital task list, prioritizing what needs your attention. As you progress through your day, take advantage of apps that offer time tracking, helping you to understand how you allocate your time, and where adjustments might be needed. These insights can guide you in refining your routines, making them more aligned with your goals and energy levels.

Beyond task management, technology offers solutions for digital decluttering. Automated file- organizing tools can sort documents into designated folders, reducing the chaos of a cluttered desktop. Imagine opening your computer to find neatly arranged files, each in its rightful place. This order extends to your digital life, minimizing the stress of searching for lost documents or missing deadlines. Email management tools, like unroll.me, help tame inbox chaos by consolidating newsletters and managing subscriptions. By reducing digital noise, these tools create a more focused and less overwhelming digital environment. Their use not only saves time but also conserves mental energy, allowing you to direct your focus toward more meaningful tasks.

As you incorporate these digital tools, remember that technology is a support system, not a replacement for your efforts. Each app or tool should enhance your natural organizational tendencies, making tasks more manageable and less daunting. Experiment with different options to find what resonates with you, adapting features to suit your unique needs. The key is to create a digital ecosystem that aligns with your lifestyle, offering both structure and flexibility. In doing so, you empower yourself to take charge of your life, transforming potential chaos into calm and order. Technology, when used wisely, becomes an ally in your pursuit of productivity and organization.

6.5 BUILD CONFIDENCE THROUGH ORGANIZATION: FEEL EMPOWERED

Imagine walking into a room where everything is lined up perfectly, each item in its place, and feeling a surge of pride. Organization isn't just about tidiness; it's a powerful confidence booster. When you successfully organize, you gain a sense of control over your environment. This control translates into self-assurance, reinforcing the belief that you can manage other areas of your life as well. Each small success in organizing builds upon the last, creating a foundation of achievement that lifts your spirits. It's like completing a puzzle, where each piece finds its place, forming a complete picture. As you organize, you see tangible results of your efforts, which boosts your self-esteem, empowering you to take on new challenges. This empowerment echoes in your actions, affecting how you approach tasks and interact with others, fostering a positive cycle of confidence and capability.

To build confidence in your organizational abilities, start by reflecting on past successes. Think back to times when you tackled a particularly messy space and emerged victorious. What were the strategies that worked for you? Reflect on how you felt once the task was completed. These memories can serve as reminders of your ability to succeed, even when you are faced with chaos. Use these reflections to motivate your future efforts, knowing that you have overcome similar challenges before. Setting and achieving incremental goals is another effective strategy. Break organizing tasks into smaller, manageable steps. Each completed step becomes a victory, reinforcing your confidence. As you accomplish these goals, take a moment to acknowledge your progress. This practice not only builds momentum, but it also strengthens your belief in your organizing skills. Small achievements lead to larger successes, creating a cycle of confidence that fuels further action.

Celebrating organizational milestones is essential for maintaining your motivation and reinforcing your confidence. Consider hosting a declutter celebration when you reach significant organizing goals. Invite friends or family to share in your success, transforming a solitary task into a communal achievement. This celebration doesn't have to be extravagant. A simple gathering, or a favorite meal, can suffice. The key is to recognize and reward your efforts, creating positive associations with organizing. These celebrations serve as tangible acknowledgments of your progress which can inspire you to continue. By celebrating milestones, you reinforce the idea that your hard work deserves recognition, boosting your confidence and motivation.

Mack's Story: From Chaos to Confidence

Mack, a 35-year-old Project Manager, had always considered himself creative, but hopelessly disorganized. Diagnosed with ADHD in his teens, he chalked up his messy life to the way his brain worked.

Struggles:

1. **Time Management:** His work deadlines often felt impossible, and his apartment was cluttered.
2. **Disorganized:** He didn't pay bills on time, missed commitments with family, friends and at work.
3. **Felt Overwhelmed:** He had unfinished projects at home and work that put pressure on him and no plan to get them finished.

Turning Point: One day, after a particularly stressful week, he forgot his parent's anniversary dinner and missed a major client deadline. Mack broke down. He realized that his current way of living was not sustainable. He loved his creativity, but he hated how disorganization made him feel like he was failing.

Changes Mack Made:

Mack joined an online ADHD support group. Through the group, he met Tim, a coach specializing in helping people with ADHD organize their lives. Tim introduced Mack to a few simple principles:

1. **Prioritized Goal Sheet:** Mack started keeping a Goal Sheet where he could jot down ideas, tasks, and reminders as they popped into his head and then prioritized them with the ABC Method.
2. **Time Blocking:** He learned to structure his day with blocks of time for creative work, admin tasks, and rest.
3. **Declutter Blasts:** Tim encouraged Mack to declutter his space for just 15 minutes a day, focusing on one small area at a time.

Results: At first, Mack doubted that these simple changes could make a difference, but within weeks, he began to see results. His Prioritizing Goal Sheet became his lifeline. He no longer worried about forgetting important tasks because they were all in one place. Time blocking helped him tackle projects without feeling overwhelmed.

The biggest surprise was how much decluttering his space freed up his mental energy. When he saw his once-cluttered desk clear, he felt a sense of pride and control. Mack even started setting up an evening reset, taking five minutes to prepare for the next day by organizing his space and reviewing his task list.

Fast-forward six months, and Mack's life looked completely different. He landed his dream client, thanks to his newfound ability to manage deadlines confidently. He rekindled friendships that he had neglected, because now he had the mental bandwidth to attend social events. Most importantly, Mack stopped viewing his ADHD as a weakness. Instead, he saw it as part of his unique wiring, which he could work with, rather than against.

Mack's transformation wasn't about becoming a perfectionist or living by rigid schedules; it was about learning small, sustainable ways to organize his life, and that honored his creativity and ADHD.

Organization is more than a skill; it's a tool for empowerment. Each step you take toward creating order strengthens your confidence and capabilities. The achievements you make in organization echo throughout your life, influencing how you approach challenges and opportunities. By embracing organization, you empower yourself to take charge, transforming chaos into calm and uncertainty into confidence. This journey of organization is a journey of empowerment, where each success builds upon the last, leading to a life of fulfillment and capability.

7

BUILD LONG-LASTING HABITS

7.1 HABIT FORMATION: TECHNIQUES FOR LASTING CHANGE

Building lasting habits, especially for those grappling with ADHD, hinges on understanding how habits are formed. At the core lies the habit loop, a simple yet powerful cycle consisting of a cue, routine, and reward. Picture this: a cue triggers a behavior, the routine follows, and a reward reinforces it. This loop repeats, embedding the habit into your daily life. Consistency and repetition are crucial. They transform new actions into automatic responses, much like tying your shoes without thinking. Your brain thrives on patterns By leveraging this, you can create habits that stick. Consistency doesn't mean perfection, but rather, the commitment to keep trying, even when setbacks occur. This commitment builds resilience and reinforces the habit loop, making each repetition easier than the last.

Start with small, manageable changes. Think of them as the first stepping stones across a river. By making these initial steps achievable, you set yourself up for success. Once you do your **Room-By-Room Inventory,** instead of tackling the room that feels the most overwhelming, choose the least. You want the task to feel important, yet feasible. For example: choose the entryway closet because it is small, can be easily organized in thirty minutes, and it will give you instant gratification. Check this off your **Goal Tracker**, take a picture and move on to the next room or part of a room on your list. This gradual progression allows you to adapt and grow without feeling overwhelmed. As small changes accumulate, they lead to meaningful transformation, providing a sense of accomplishment and motivation to continue.

We completed the **Personal Habit Tracking Time Audit**. The goal of this audit was to show us our current habits. Remember the section on **Habit Stacking**? You tie a current habit to a new habit to signal your brain to initiate a routine. Recognizing and using these cues can simplify habit formation, reducing your mental effort required to initiate a habit. Over time, these cues become ingrained, making habits feel like a natural part of your routine. They provide structure and predictability. You don't decide, you "just do it".

7.2 MOTIVATION FLUCTUATIONS: JONTY'S ADVICE

Imagine waking up, feeling a surge of eagerness to tackle your goals, only to have that drive vanish by midday. This is the unpredictable nature of motivation, especially for those with ADHD. Motivation isn't constant. It ebbs and flows, swayed by mood, energy levels, and even external circumstances. Some days you feel unstoppable, while on others, even the simplest task can feel monumental. We all have times of low motivation. Understanding this variability and how it ties to habits is the key to managing your life effectively. I will never forget a conversation I had with my friend Jonty just a few years ago. We were talking specifically about exercise, and I was telling him that I used to have so much motivation, and at that point in my life, I just didn't. He looked me straight in the eyes and gave me the best advice about motivation I've ever received. He said calmly and pointedly, "Amy, motivation will always come and go, but discipline rules everything". You see, it wasn't a motivation problem. I had slacked on the habits that create discipline. I was relying on motivation, which will consistently fail. That one conversation changed the way I looked at everything about habits from that point forward.

You see, when I was in college, I was very disciplined. I employed all of the things we talk about in this book to create great habits. I was a 3-sport athlete, worked as a janitor to pay for my schooling, and took a full course-load every semester. I ran every day to stay in shape for my sports in addition to attending the mandatory practices for the various sports. I had very little space in my dorm, so I was forced to be organized with my personal belongings. I had very little time, so I also organized my time efficiently. I look back on it now and am truly amazed at how high functioning I was. I don't remember the word "motivation" ever passing my lips. I had the "Just Do It" mentality, and I had created systems to excel in all that I chose to spend my time doing.

After graduating, I got a full-time job, got married, had kids and took on many other roles. One thing that stayed constant through all those changes in my life was exercise. The mode of exercise changed throughout the years: running, workout classes, spin, golf, pilates, yoga, etc. Did I have more motivation when I was younger? You bet your booty I did. Did I keep showing up for myself even if I wasn't motivated? Also a resounding, YES. I think I just never recognized the level of discipline and good habits that I had had all those years of working out. Jonty made me take a hard look at myself and my habits and pat myself on the back for the years and years of consistent effort that I had put in. I just needed to shift my focus back to habits and not motivation.

During times of high motivation, it's crucial to capitalize on this energy. These periods are when building and reinforcing habits can be the most effective. Use this time to tackle more challenging tasks or establish new routines. It's like riding a wave; the momentum can carry you further than you'd expect, however, when motivation wanes, habits and discipline will take you the rest of the way to the completion of the task.

7.3 ACCOUNTABILITY SYSTEMS: HELPING YOU STAY ON TRACK

Imagine having a safety net that supports your climb toward better habits. Accountability systems can be that safety net, enhancing your consistency and success. Whether through peer accountability groups, or professional coaching, these systems provide a framework of support and encouragement. In a busy world, it's easy to lose sight of personal goals amidst daily chaos. Accountability acts as a steady reminder, nudging you back on track when you veer off course. It transforms the solitary journey of habit formation into a shared experience, where motivation is bolstered by the presence and support of others.

There are many types of accountability systems that can suit your needs. Buddy systems are one example, where you partner with someone who shares similar goals. This mutual support creates a sense of camaraderie, as you cheer each other on through challenges and celebrate victories together. Online forums also offer community support, connecting you with individuals who understand your struggles and triumphs. These platforms provide a space to share experiences, exchange advice, and find solace in knowing that you are not alone. Both buddy systems and online communities foster an environment of shared purpose, where encouragement flows freely, and accountability feels less like a burden, and more like a shared commitment.

Choosing the right accountability partner is crucial for success. Look for someone whose goals and values align with yours. This alignment ensures a mutual understanding and a cohesive approach to habit-building. Reliable and consistent communication is another key factor. Frequent check-ins, whether through text messages, calls, or in-person meetings, can keep the momentum alive and provide opportunities to discuss progress and setbacks. Your partner should be someone you trust, who can offer constructive feedback and encouragement without judgment. This relationship becomes a pillar of support, reinforcing your resolve and reminding you of your capabilities.

In today's digital age, technology can play a vital role in accountability. Shared digital calendars allow you and your accountability partner to track deadlines and milestones, ensuring that both parties remain informed and engaged. These calendars provide visual reminders of upcoming tasks and goals, reducing the likelihood of procrastination. Task-sharing apps, like Asana or Trello, facilitate collaboration by organizing tasks and tracking progress in real-time. These tools create transparency and foster communication, allowing you to see at a glance what's been accomplished, and what still needs attention. By integrating technology into your accountability system, you streamline the process while enhancing your ability to stay on course.

Accountability systems are not just about checking off tasks. They offer a deeper connection to your goals, transforming them into shared endeavors that foster growth and resilience. You become part of a network that celebrates your successes and supports you through challenges. This connection provides a sense of belonging, making the often daunting process of habit formation feel less isolated. With accountability, your goals become more than just aspirations, they become achievable realities supported by a web of encouragement and shared commitment.

7.4 ADHD COACHES

If you don't feel like you are comfortable finding an accountability buddy, you could hire an ADHD Coach. An ADHD coach assists people with ADHD build effective strategies to address challenges and manage their lives better. They help their clients develop structure, skills, and action plans to tackle any responsibilities or goals made more difficult by ADHD symptoms. Every person is walking their own path. No two individuals will have the same experiences. This book is merely a guide to help you find your own path to success. Here are several reasons why someone with ADHD might benefit from working with an accountability coach:

1. **External Motivation**
   - People with ADHD often struggle with intrinsic motivation, especially for tasks that feel boring or overwhelming.
   - An accountability coach provides external motivation by setting deadlines, checking progress, and celebrating successes.
2. **Breaking Down Overwhelming Tasks**
   - ADHD can make large tasks feel insurmountable. A coach helps break these into smaller, manageable steps.
   - This makes starting and completing tasks less intimidating.
3. **Creating and Maintaining Structure**
   - Many individuals with ADHD struggle to create consistent routines or stick to plans.

- A coach helps establish structure and ensures it's realistic and sustainable.
4. **Regular Check-Ins**
    - ADHD brains often require frequent reminders and check-ins to stay on track.
    - Knowing that someone will follow up can increase follow-through on commitments.
5. **Developing Strategies for Time Management**
    - ADHD frequently leads to poor time management and difficulty estimating how long tasks will take.
    - Coaches teach techniques like time-blocking, using timers, or scheduling buffer time between activities.
6. **Building Self-Confidence**
    - Chronic struggles with ADHD often erode self-esteem due to missed deadlines, forgotten tasks, or a sense of failure.
    - A coach provides encouragement, reinforces strengths, and helps rebuild confidence by focusing on achievements.
7. **Accountability Without Judgment**
    - ADHD can bring feelings of shame or guilt about being disorganized or procrastinating.
    - A coach offers support in a judgment-free environment, fostering growth rather than criticism.
8. **Improving Focus**
    - A coach helps identify specific distractions and create personalized strategies to minimize them.
    - Techniques like prioritization, environmental adjustments, and focusing tools (e.g., Pomodoro timers) are often introduced.
9. **Tailored Goal-Setting**
    - People with ADHD can struggle to set realistic, actionable goals or follow through on them.

- Coaches work collaboratively to set achievable goals that align with personal values and needs.

10. **Overcoming Procrastination**
    - ADHD often leads to putting off tasks until the last minute, which can result in stress or subpar outcomes.
    - A coach helps create proactive systems to combat procrastination, like scheduling small steps over time or pairing tasks with rewards.

11. **Providing a Nonjudgmental Sounding Board**
    - ADHD individuals often have creative, unconventional ideas but may struggle to organize or act on them.
    - A coach listens, offers feedback, and helps transform ideas into actionable plans.

12. **Encouraging Follow-Through**
    - Many ADHD individuals start projects with enthusiasm but struggle to finish them.
    - A coach helps track progress and provides the consistency needed to see tasks through to completion.

13. **Addressing Emotional Dysregulation**
    - ADHD can involve intense emotional responses or difficulties regulating emotions.
    - Coaches provide support and perspective during challenging moments, helping clients stay grounded and focused.

14. **Customizing Solutions**
    - ADHD brains are unique; what works for one person might not work for another.
    - A coach tailors solutions to fit the individual's preferences, strengths, and lifestyle.

15. **Reducing Decision Fatigue**
    - ADHD can make even simple decisions feel exhausting.
    - A coach simplifies this by narrowing options or helping clients create default choices for recurring situations.

An accountability coach serves as a partner in navigating the challenges of ADHD while celebrating progress and empowering individuals to thrive. For many, the relationship with a coach becomes a crucial element in achieving their goals and finding balance in life.

ADHD coaching alone (or in combination with treatment) can positively impact your task performance, social skills, and emotions. But the key to reaping these benefits is finding a professional coach who understands your needs and goals.

If you need help finding a coach for adults, you can go to https://add.org/how-to-find-an-adhd-coach/. If you are looking for a coach for your teens there's a site called Coachbit.com that helps teens learn how to work with their ADHD and learn habits to help them build a great future.

7.5 REAL-LIFE SUCCESS STORIES: INSPIRATION FROM OTHERS

Sarah, an ADHD Mother Creating Order from Chaos

Sarah is a 35-year-old mother of three children, aged 5, 8, and 11. Diagnosed with ADHD in her late twenties, Sarah had always struggled with staying organized. After becoming a mother, the challenges intensified. Toys piled up in the living room, school permission slips were perpetually misplaced, and dinner often became a last-minute scramble. Sarah frequently felt overwhelmed and frustrated, believing she was failing as a parent.

Struggles:

1. **Overwhelmed by Clutter:** Sarah found herself constantly battling clutter. Her kids' toys, clothes, and homework

were always in disarray, making it difficult to find what was needed.
2. **Time Management Woes:** She missed appointments and often underestimated how long tasks would take, leading to a perpetual feeling of being rushed.
3. **Emotional Burnout:** The constant sense of chaos led Sarah to feel defeated and ashamed. She began to lose confidence in her ability to manage her household.

Turning Point:

One day, Sarah forgot about her youngest child's kindergarten recital, a moment she had been looking forward to, but had misplaced on her mental to-do list. That experience was the wake-up call she needed. Sarah realized that to support her family and herself, she had to create systems that worked with her ADHD, and not against it.

The Changes Sarah Made:

1. **Task Division:** Sarah realized that organizing in broad categories overwhelmed her. Instead, she adopted task division-breaking a job down into smaller parts. For example:
    - A labeled bin for each child's toys.
    - A designated "launchpad" by the front door where backpacks, shoes, and coats were kept for quick morning exits.
    - A small, clear file box for school papers, separated by child.
2. **Visual Cues:** Recognizing that out of sight often meant out of mind for her, Sarah implemented visual systems:
    - A large whiteboard calendar in the kitchen with color-coded entries for each family member.

- Open shelving for frequently used kitchen items.
    - A "priority box" on her desk for critical items like bills and school notices.
3. **Time Management Tools:** Sarah began using a visual timer for chores and tasks, breaking them into manageable 15-minute chunks. She also started setting alarms on her phone for daily routines like starting dinner or picking up her kids.
4. **Delegation:** Realizing she didn't have to do everything herself, Sarah involved her kids in small, age-appropriate chores. For example, the 8-year-old was responsible for sorting clean laundry, while the 11-year-old helped with meal prep.
5. **Grace and Flexibility:** Sarah worked on letting go of perfectionism. She learned to prioritize what mattered most and accept that some days would still be messy. She started attending a local ADHD support group, which provided her with community and encouragement.

Results:

Sarah's home became more manageable. Mornings were smoother because everyone knew where their belongings were. Sarah felt more in control of her schedule, and the kids began to thrive in their more structured environment. More importantly, Sarah felt empowered, capable, and confident as a mother.

Emily, an ADHD Graphic Designer taking control of her time

Emily, a graphic designer diagnosed with ADHD in her teens, now in her late twenties, found herself constantly overwhelmed by the chaos in her apartment and studio. Despite her creativity, maintaining a routine cleaning and decluttering schedule seemed insurmountable.

Struggles:

- **Maintaining a Routine:** She worked from home and had no set schedule. Getting even the smallest task done was difficult because she constantly felt overwhelmed by all of the things that needed to be done and the clutter surrounding her home and studio.
- **Time Management Woes:** She did not schedule her time, and felt that doing so would stifle her creativity.
- **Embarrassment and Isolation**: Her home was in a constant state of disarray. She was embarrassed to invite friends to her home, so she isolated herself, which made things even harder.

Turning Point:

Her sister came to town and needed a place to stay, giving her very little notice. Her sister was appalled at the clutter and mess, so she had a heart-to-heart conversation with her, asking her if she needed help. Emily got angry at first, but then realized that her sister was right. She did need help.

The Changes Emily Made:

1. **Teamwork and a Written Plan**: Emily and her sister worked for a solid day making a written plan, and then they started decluttering the house, one room at a time. They sorted, bought clear bins, and labeled everything. They made great progress and Emily felt confident that she could move forward on her own.

2. **Task Division**: Emily decided to adopt an incremental approach to habit-building. She broke down big tasks into smaller, more manageable tasks, such as cleaning the house. She is now making her bed each morning, decluttering one area of the home for 15 minutes throughout the day and then organizing her workspace for just 5 minutes at the end of each day. Emily found that these small steps reduced her stress levels, and slowly built the foundation for more significant habits.
3. **Planner**: Emily got a planner, and now schedules her work day and time for organizing and cleaning. She also schedules time for herself.
4. **Journaling**: She incorporated consistent self-reflection practices while journaling her progress weekly, which helped her to recognize patterns, and adjust her strategies. This process not only transformed her living space, but it also boosted her confidence so that she could invite friends to her home, and enabled her to take on more complex organizational challenges.

Results:

Emily's home and workspace is more calm and inviting now, and she feels that she has more control of her time. She is more productive, and has the emotional space to be creative and spend more time with her friends.

Alex, a college student athlete learning to manage his life.

Alex had a mother that took care of many daily tasks for him. He was diagnosed with ADHD in high school, and his mom felt that doing things for him was helping him, so he could still play sports, which meant that he never learned how to manage himself.

Struggles:

1. **Irresponsibility:** Alex did not use a planner, so he would forget his assignments, or he would write things down on a paper that would get lost. He would turn in assignments late, or not at all.
2. **Punctuality:** He would oversleep and show up late to classes and to his job. He would play video games until late in the night, so he was tired all day.
3. **Disorganization:** His dorm room was smelly, dirty, and cluttered, so he also struggled to find his belongings.

Turning Point: Alex's grades had slipped so far that the coach gave him a warning that if he didn't raise his grades, he would be off the team and lose his scholarship. He realized that he needed to change. If he was going to stay on the team and have a bright future, he needed to figure out how to manage his life on his own.

Changes Made:

1. **Digital Calendar and Planner:** He downloaded a planner app that many of his teammates were using, and he started using it. He now adds all of his assignments and due dates into his calendar and app. He created a study schedule, dividing his workload into smaller, manageable segments. By dedicating specific times for each subject, he could focus better and avoid burnout. His key to success was consistent adaptation. As the semester progressed, he regularly reviewed and adjusted his study plan based upon what was working, and what wasn't. He has also decided that he only plays video games if he first sets a timer. When the timer goes off, he is done playing.

2. **Sort:** Since he was in a small dorm room, he started with pulling everything out, and sorting through it. He used a pitch, keep, or donate method. He then put his belongings away in a specific place that he designated so that now, each item now has a home.
3. **Habit Stacking:** He stacks habits he already has with new habits. He takes the old habit of brushing his teeth, and then adds the new habit of spraying and wiping down the bathroom counters. His old habit of playing video games is now stacked with doing his laundry.
4. **Scheduled Cleaning:** He added cleaning time into his planner. He cleans and organizes for 15 minutes every day.
5. **Timer and Alarms:** He uses his alarm to wake up on time, and chooses to set a timer when gaming and cleaning/organizing.

Results:

Alex's life is completely different now. His assignments are completed, his grades have improved, his dorm room is no longer smelly or dirty. He can find his belongings easily, as they all have a specified place. He is punctual, and has a more balanced lifestyle.

These stories illustrate that overcoming habit challenges with ADHD is possible, and the strategies used by Sarah, Emily, and Alex can be adapted to fit your unique context. Whether you start with small, consistent actions, or by routinely evaluating your methods, the lessons from these stories offer a roadmap for your success. Consider what simple changes you can implement today. Perhaps you start with organizing one drawer, or by setting up a reminder for a recurring task. The key is to tailor these strategies to your life, ensuring that they resonate with your goals and challenges. As you make progress, remember that self-reflection is your ally. Regularly check in with yourself to assess what is working, and where adjustments are needed. This practice not only keeps you accountable but also fosters a growth mindset, encouraging continuous improvement.

Sharing your success stories can be just as powerful as learning from others. Your experiences hold the potential to inspire those who face similar challenges. Participate in online communities where you can connect and share your journey with others who understand the unique struggles of ADHD. These platforms provide a supportive environment where you can celebrate victories, seek advice, and offer encouragement. Local support groups also offer opportunities for face-to-face interactions, creating a sense of camaraderie and a shared purpose. By engaging with these communities, you not only reinforce your own progress, but you can also contribute to a collective pool of knowledge and inspiration. Your story might be the catalyst for someone else's transformation, proving that with the right strategies and support, lasting change is within reach.

7.6 ADAPT STRATEGIES OVER TIME: FLEXIBILITY IN HABITS

Life is anything but static. As you navigate through different phases, your circumstances, responsibilities, and even your personal goals will transform. This ever-changing landscape demands flexibility, especially when it comes to habit development. Imagine your routines as a river constantly flowing and adapting to the terrain that it encounters. Clinging to rigid habits in a dynamic life can lead to frustration and failure. When you allow your habits to evolve with your life changes, you can create a system that supports sustainable growth. For instance, a new job might require you to adjust your morning routine to accommodate an earlier start. Or perhaps a shift in family dynamics means reallocating time for personal care. Recognizing these changes and adapting accordingly is vital. It's about being in tune with your needs and making conscious adjustments that align with your current reality. This flexibility ensures that your habits remain effective, relevant, and supportive, rather than becoming another source of stress.

To ensure that your habits are effective and aligned with your goals, regular evaluation is necessary. Consider setting aside time each month to review your habits. Ask yourself if they are still serving your objectives, or if they need to be tweaked. This practice, like a maintenance check, helps you identify what's working and what isn't. Reflection plays a crucial role in this process. Dive into the deeper reason behind each habit. Does it resonate with your core values and contribute to your overarching goals? For example: if you started exercising for stress relief, but it has become just another box to tick off your list, it might be time to explore new activities that reignite your motivation and joy. By being honest with yourself about your needs and adjusting your habits accordingly, you can maintain a system that not only supports your goals, but also aligns with your evolving life circumstances.

Adopting a flexible approach to habit formation offers numerous benefits. First and foremost, it reduces stress and frustration. When you allow yourself permission to adapt, you remove the pressure of perfection. This adaptability fosters resilience, as you learn to navigate the ebbs and flows of life without feeling defeated by setbacks. A flexible mindset encourages exploration and experimentation, providing the freedom to try new methods and discard what doesn't work. This openness leads to sustainable habit formation, as you continuously refine your approach, ensuring that it remains relevant and effective. By embracing change and viewing it as an opportunity, rather than a challenge, you can cultivate an environment where habits thrive, evolve, and support your personal growth.

To foster an adaptive mindset, consider incorporating growth mindset exercises into your routine. These practices encourage you to view challenges as opportunities for learning and development. Begin by reframing setbacks as valuable experiences that provide insights to guide future actions. For example; if you miss a day in your routine, instead of viewing it as a failure, see it as a chance to identify potential obstacles and develop strategies to overcome them. Another exercise involves reflecting on past achievements and the lessons learned along the way. Acknowledge your progress and the adaptability that got you to where you are today. These reflections reinforce the belief that you are capable of growth and change. By cultivating a mindset open to adaptation, you empower yourself to navigate life's uncertainties with confidence and resilience, ensuring that your habits remain a source of strength and support.

7.7 REWARD SYSTEMS: ENCOURAGING CONSISTENT PROGRESS

Imagine that you're working hard to establish a new habit, and every day you make progress feels like a small victory. But what keeps you going when the initial excitement fades? That's where the power of rewards comes into play. Rewards are a cornerstone of habit formation because they reinforce positive behavior, making it more likely that you will repeat it. Your brain responds to rewards by releasing dopamine, the feel-good neurotransmitter, creating a strong association between the action and the pleasure it brings. This biological response is why immediate gratification can be so enticing. It provides a quick hit of pleasure that makes the effort feel worthwhile. However, delayed gratification often builds a deeper sense of satisfaction, as the anticipation and eventual reward makes the journey feel more rewarding. Balancing these two forms of gratification is crucial. They both play unique roles in sustaining your motivation and helping you to achieve your goals.

Let's explore some effective reward systems that can help to keep you motivated. For daily accomplishments, consider small treats that bring you joy without derailing your progress. This could be as simple as enjoying a favorite snack or taking a relaxing break after completing a task. These small rewards act as regular encouragement, keeping your spirits high and your momentum going. For long-term goals, larger rewards can provide a powerful incentive. Imagine treating yourself to a weekend getaway, or a new gadget, after reaching a significant milestone. These bigger rewards can serve as a beacon, guiding you through challenges and helping you to maintain focus on the bigger picture. The key is to choose rewards that genuinely motivate you, making the effort feel worthwhile, and the achievement, all the sweeter.

Aligning rewards with your values is essential to ensure that they support your habit goals. Material rewards can be tempting, but experiential (based on experience) ones hold more weight in reinforcing the value of your efforts. Consider rewards that resonate with your personal interests and aspirations. If you value quality time with loved ones, reward yourself with a special outing or dinner with friends. These experiences not only provide immediate joy, but they also reinforce the deeper motivations behind your habits. By choosing rewards that align with your values, you create a system that not only motivates, but also enriches your life, making each milestone feel meaningful and connected to your personal growth.

Maintaining a balanced reward system is crucial to avoid over-reliance on external incentives. Periodically review the effectiveness of your rewards to ensure that they remain motivational and relevant. If you find that a particular reward no longer excites you, don't hesitate to adjust it. As habits become ingrained, your need for external motivation may decrease, allowing you to shift the focus from extrinsic to intrinsic rewards. This transition reflects a deeper commitment to the habit itself, where the satisfaction of completion becomes the reward. By staying attuned to your motivations and adjusting rewards as needed, you can maintain a dynamic system that continues to support your habit development, while fostering a sense of autonomy and fulfillment.

KEEP THE MOMENTUM GOING

Well, here we are; at the finish line! You've made it through *ADHD Organizing Made Easy*, and I hope that it has left you feeling inspired, equipped, and maybe even a little fired up, to create calm in your home by organizing your life in short, doable bursts! But before you head off to conquer the world, I have one last favor to ask.

Would you mind sharing your thoughts about this book?

Your honest opinion and *your* unique perspective can help others just like you to discover the same support, insights, and encouragement. When you leave a review on Amazon, you're not just jotting down some words; you're handing over a road map to someone who might be feeling as stuck as you once were.

Why It Matters

The world of ADHD thrives when we share what we've learned. By leaving a review, you'll show other people who feel overwhelmed with clutter, that they're not alone, and that the answers they're searching for are just a few pages away.

It doesn't have to be long or fancy, just tell the truth. What did you love? What surprised you? How has the book helped you to move closer to your goals? Every little bit counts.

Ready to Help Someone Else?

It's super simple:

1. Go to: **https://www.amazon.com/review/create-review/?ie=UTF8&channel=glance-detail&asin=B0DRW9FCRP or scan the QR code to leave your review on Amazon.**
2. Share your honest opinion. (Seriously, even a sentence or two can make a huge difference!)
3. Hit submit and pat yourself on the back. You have just helped keep ADHD Organizing alive!

Thank You

This book is just the start of something bigger. By sharing your experience, you're helping to keep the passion for organizing going strong, and showing others that change is possible. You're a vital part of this journey, not just for me, but for every reader who follows in your footsteps.

With gratitude and excitement for all you'll achieve,

Amy Miller

P.S. Don't be shy. If there's something you loved, or a way that this book helped you, I'd love to hear your story. Reach out at [your email address] anytime!

CONCLUSION

Let's reiterate what you have learned in the previous chapters:

- We took a **Room-by-Room Inventory**. We noted Hot Spots that needed attention and we noted things we liked about each room such as "great natural light", etc.
- We created a **Goal Sheet**. This is an evolving document where we set goals based on our room-by-room inventory.
- We completed a **Habit Tracking Time Audit** to discover our habits, how we are spending our time, and how we could improve on our processes.
- We learned about the **Short Burst** technique where you set a timer for 30 minutes and work solid until the timer goes off. Then you take a break for 5 minutes to help keep you motivated and on task throughout the work day.
- We learned how to **Prioritize** using the ABC method and how to apply this to our Goal Sheet.
- We learned about **Task Dividing** Breaking down tasks into manageable parts.

- We learned about **Habit Stacking** - Tying a current positive habit with a new habit to make it easier to follow through.
- We learned about the **Decluttering Blast** technique - Taking one of the goals from your Goal sheet, setting a timer for 15 minutes, and then working hard to complete the task within the designated time.
- We learned about the **One Year Rule** and **Emotional Decluttering**.
- We learned **Practical Tips** for every room.
- We learned about **Digital Decluttering**.
- We learned about **Streamlined Systems** Creating a flow that is simple and easy to follow, that makes sense for the space, and in turn, becomes natural to maintain daily.
- We learned about **Optimizing your Workspace** and **Overcoming Procrastination**.
- We learned about **Motivation vs. Habits** and how to stay on track.

As you reach the end of this journey, take a moment to reflect on the path you've traversed. From the initial chaos, to a newfound sense of order, this book can be your guide to navigate the unique challenges and opportunities that come with organizing, while living with ADHD. We started by understanding the ADHD brain, acknowledging its impact on organization, and recognizing the creativity and innovation it can bring.

Throughout the chapters, the focus has been on creating a personalized organizational plan. It is essential that your strategies reflect who you are, catering to your specific needs. This isn't a one-size-fits-all approach. Instead, it's about finding methods that resonate with you, making organizing not just a task, but a part of your lifestyle.

Time management and prioritization have been core themes, crucial for harnessing your potential. The techniques discussed, such as Time Blocking and the Pomodoro Technique, are designed to help you gain control over your schedule. By prioritizing tasks effectively, you can transform overwhelming lists into manageable actions, ensuring your productivity and peace of mind.

Managing clutter, both physical and digital, is another cornerstone of this book. You've learned actionable steps to declutter your space, while making room for what truly matters. Whether it's a quick declutter blast, or a comprehensive digital cleanup, these strategies aim to reduce stress and enhance your environment.

A productive environment plays a pivotal role in supporting your organizing efforts. A well-organized setting not only boosts productivity, but can also reduce stress. By making simple adjustments in your home or workspace, you can create an atmosphere that nurtures focus and clarity.

Building lasting habits is fundamental to sustaining the progress you've made. The techniques shared, like habit stacking and monitoring progress, are tools to help you form habits that align with your goals. These habits become the framework that supports your organizational aspirations.

Integrating organization into your daily life is the ultimate goal. It's about weaving these strategies seamlessly into your routines, making organization second nature. The key is consistency; adapting the methods to fit your evolving life circumstances.

Now, I invite you to reflect on your organizing journey. Set personal goals based on what you've learned, and take the first steps in implementing these strategies. Remember that organization is not a destination, it's a lifelong practice. Stay committed and adaptable as life changes. Your journey doesn't end here; it evolves with you.

I'm confident in your ability to transform your life through organization. You have the tools, the knowledge, and the potential to achieve lasting change. As you continue on this path, know that you are not alone. This book is a testament to your strength and determination. Keep moving forward, embracing the organized life that you deserve.

BONUS: PRINTABLES

So where do we go from here? Let's put all that we learned into practice. Here is a link that takes you to all the printables I've created for you to start your organizational journey and help you stay on the path to an organized life. Using the printables is simple. Just write on the printouts and post them where you can see them until the task is completed. This is where you can get creative with color-coding to make them visually appealing and stimulating for you. Here's to a calm and clutter-free future. Happy Organizing!

REFERENCES

Inside the ADHD Brain: Structure, Function, and Chemistry https://add.org/adhd-brain/

10 Best ADHD Organization & Management Tools in 2024 https://clickup.com/blog/adhd-organization-tools/

Calmness in Chaos: The True Measure Of A Man - Nick Kastrup https://nicklasstenderkastrup.medium.com/calmness-in-chaos-the-true-measure-of-a-man-dead-presidents-and-lessons-from-history-aa531535dd5a

33 ADHD-Friendly Ways to Get Organized - ADDitude https://www.additudemag.com/how-to-get-organized-with-adhd/

ADHD Goal Setting - Unconventional Organisation https://www.unconventionalorganisation.com/post/adhd-goal-setting

How to Organize Your Home: A Room-by-Room Guide https://www.additudemag.com/slideshows/how-to-organize-your-home-room-by-room/

6 ADHD Visual Tools Guaranteed to Make Organizing Easy https://justanorganizedhome.com/adhd-visual-tools/

ADHD Time Blindness: How to Detect It & Regain Control ... https://add.org/adhd-time-blindness/

How to Declutter: 7 Tips for ADHD Adults https://www.additudemag.com/slideshows/how-to-declutter-adhd/

Finding Freedom from Clutter: Overcoming Emotional ... https://www.therelationshipcentre.ca/finding-freedom-from-clutter-overcoming-emotional-attachments-and-resistance/

14 Proven Strategies And Tools For Year-End Digital ... - Forbes https://www.forbes.com/councils/forbeshumanresourcescouncil/2023/09/11/14-proven-strategies-and-tools-for-year-end-digital-decluttering

How To Set Up An ADHD-Friendly Organization System https://imbusybeingawesome.com/adhd-organization-system/

Clutter and Mental Health: What's the Connection? https://www.verywellmind.com/decluttering-our-house-to-cleanse-our-minds-5101511

Best Productivity Apps for Adults with ADHD: Our Top Picks https://www.additudemag.com/best-productivity-apps-adhd-adults/

How to Improve Executive Function in ADHD Adults: A Guide https://connectedspeechpathology.com/blog/how-to-improve-executive-function-in-adhd-adults

Habit Stacking: Definition, Steps, Benefits for ADHD https://www.verywellmind.com/habit-stacking-definition-steps-benefits-for-adhd-6751145

ADHD and Habits: What Helps Form Them https://marlacummins.com/adhd-and-habits-making-them-stick/

Environments and Situations that Worsen ADHD Symptoms https://www.envisionadhd.com/single-post/environments-and-situations-that-worsen-adhd-symptoms

Support Groups for Adults - ADDA https://add.org/adhd-support-groups/

Made in the USA
Columbia, SC
26 February 2025

54419225R00065